Witton Warr...

1914 - 1919

By

Anne Yuill

Published by 'Relativity'

Witton le Wear

2012

First Edition 2012

ISBN-978-0-957-125-71-1

Crown Copyright permission for reproduction of some photographs has been given by the National Archives

Printed by

Eli Press
121, Low Etherley, Bishop Auckland,
Co. Durham DL14 0HA

To the best of the authors knowledge, the information in this book is accurate but if readers wish to make comment, they can contact the author at relativity@sky.com

Further copies of this book may be obtained from the author who can be contacted by email at: relativity@sky.com
or by telephone 01388488376

Dedication

'To remember and be remembered is a special privilege'

This book is dedicated to the memory of Rosemary Woods,

a good friend, a fellow nurse,

and a lover of the history

of Witton le Wear, Co. Durham.

Other books by the author

'Biting the Bullet' published 2012

Foreword

On Remembrance Sunday 2003, I was sitting in the parish church in Witton le Wear looking at the war memorial. The church warden, Peter Mortimer stood and read out the names of the men who died during World War I.

Captain G Sadler	**Lieut. H McGuire**	**Corporal B A Randall**
Private W Allinson	**Private F W Hall**	**Private E Hogg**
Private H Langstaff	**Private G Scott**	**Private A Smith**
	Private T Stobbs	

I started to wonder who these men were. What were their first names? Where did they live? Who were their families? I made a vow there and then to try to find out their names so that the following year, their full names could be recited - the challenge began.

Another project I was involved in was the recording of the names and inscriptions on the graves in the village cemetery. Every time I visited I was distressed to find that many of the stones were in a deteriorating condition and some had fallen over and had been removed from the graveside for health and safety reasons. The local cemeteries department does not have a complete list of all the graves, so that spurred me into recording the remaining graves that could be deciphered. Rosemary Woods, to whom this book is dedicated, helped me with the transcribing and we spent many days with paper and pen recording details in the cemetery. There is now a full database of all the stones extant at 2010, and we managed to combine this with information about graves with no headstones. This information is now available for family historians and local people.

We came across four graves which named men who died during World War I and are remembered on their family's gravestones who are not named on the Witton le Wear Memorial. They are:

Alexander Richardson	**Christopher Whitton**	**John Saunders**	**Albert Dean MC**

It was interesting that as far as I know, nobody living in the village currently knew that these men were remembered in the cemetery. On further research, I also discovered another soldier, James Coates who died during World War I and had been born in Witton le Wear but moved out of the village to North Bitchburn, only four miles away, by the age of 7.

Durham County Record Office holds the Absentee Voters List recorded in October 1918 for Witton le Wear and this identifies 53 men from the village who were serving away from home and were eligible to vote in the October 1918 elections. The majority survived the war and information about them is also included.

'Witton Warriors' gives an overview of Witton le Wear in the early 1900s and focuses on the stories of the men linked to Witton le Wear during the First World War. The information on the men is as accurate as I have been able to make it. My sources have varied from personal family accounts, army records, war diaries, birth and marriage certificates, census, electoral rolls and a variety of research books and articles. When I discovered that 60% of all WWI records were destroyed in the London blitz in 1940, it was disappointing, as it meant that many of the individual service records could never be found. It does however, make it all the more gratifying when one finds that records do exist and these provide a valuable insight into what really happened to individual soldiers. It brings them to life and lifts them from being simply names on a brass plaque to become real people.

Like all research, this is an evolving process and I am sure there is more information to uncover in the future. I will be very interested in hearing from anybody who has any comments to make, other information to add or any corrections to make in the information presented. (email: relativity@sky.com)

It was my intention that readers could dip in and out of this book reading sections of particular interest: individual soldier's stories, or what it was like on the home front, or who lived where etc., rather than reading the book cover to cover. During the preparation of 'Witton Warriors' I have experienced such a wide range of emotions: surprise, happiness, anxiety, frustration, pride but mostly the recognition that this war was a waste of a whole generation. Young men sent to war never to return; many of those who returned were broken men with life changing injuries; families devastated and communities changed forever. Of the soldiers who returned, few expressed their personal account of the war and in many cases there are no lasting memorials to the fallen. Yes, there is one in stone or brass but as time passes, generations die and families move away to live in other parts of the world, grandparents are unable to tell future generations about these ancestors.

There are people currently living in the Witton le Wear parish who may never have seen the war memorial in the church. The men who died are in danger of being forgotten apart from one day a year when the Remembrance Day Sunday service is held on the Sunday nearest to the 11th November. 'Witton Warriors' will do its part to perpetuate the memory of the men of Witton le Wear who served their King, their country and their communities, and who gave their lives for the freedom of us all.

Anne Yuill   May 2012

Acknowledgements

This book has taken many years in its planning and research. I need to acknowledge many people for their support. My husband and family have allowed me to follow my passion and have encouraged me all the way.

Thanks are given to Durham County Councillor Anita Savory, who made available generous a grant to pay for some of the publishing costs for this book from her neighbourhood budget. This will allow every household, school and business in Witton le Wear parish to receive a copy of this book free of charge which will ensure the legacy will live on in perpetuity. Witton le Wear Parish Council have also offered their support for this work.

Through my friend Rosemary to whom this book is dedicated, I became personally acquainted with two of the families of soldiers mentioned within the book. The late Stan Scott was a nephew of George Walton Scott and Peggy Selzler is the granddaughter of Joe Jackson. Stan and Peggy both gave permission for their information to be used in the book. Joe's family have kindly shared his personal journal from 1915-1916 and some photographs which tell his story and that of many other soldiers, better than I could ever do. Brenda Rowland and her family who live at West End visited Bertram Randall's grave and shared their photographs. Clive and George Gillard shared information and photographs about their grandfather Walter Gillard who survived the war. The headmistress at Wolsingham Grammar School supplied the photographs of Alec Richardson and Harry Langstaff. Peter and Norma Mortimer reviewed the Absentee Voters List and provided some additional information.

The records held at the National Archives, in Kew and various military museums throughout the country have been a valuable resource and their curators helpful when questions have come to the fore. Durham County Record Office archives have been an excellent resource when it came to finding out about the history of the actual memorial and accessing the Absentee Voters List. The North East War Memorial Project has inspired and informed providing good background material.

Lastly but not least, my husband Kelso has been my inspiration, my military advisor, proof reader and has provided the motivation at times when enthusiasm waned. Without him, this book would not have been written.

Contents

War Memorial in the Parish Church of St Philip and St James, Witton le Wear
(Author's collection)

The Witton le Wear WWI War Memorial
(Author's collection)

Parish Church of St Philip and St James, Witton le Wear c1910
(Author's collection)

Witton le Wear from western end of village c1920
(Author's collection)

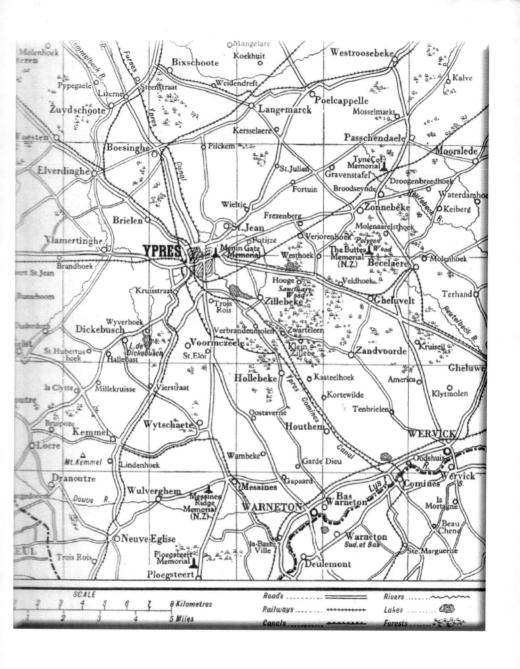

Map of Ypres area c1918
(Swinton collection)

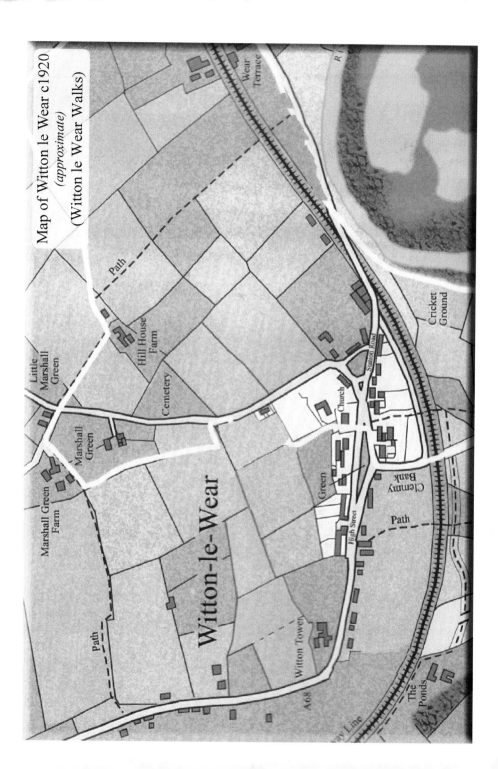

Map of Witton le Wear c1920
(approximate)
(Witton le Wear Walks)

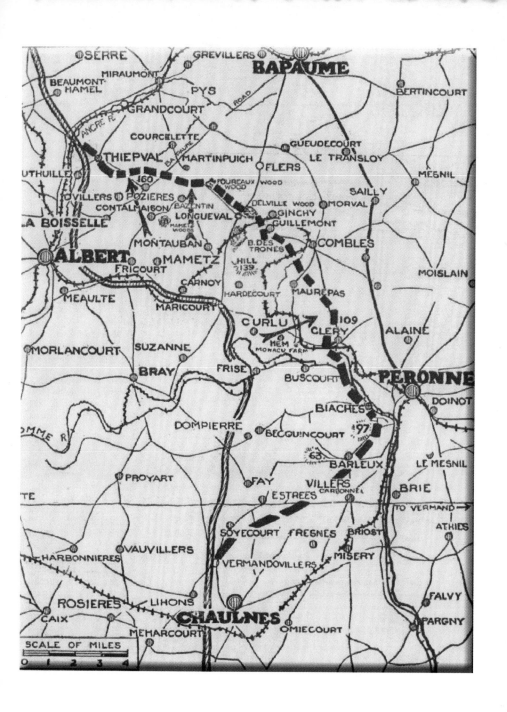

Map of Somme area c1918
(Somme Tourist Board)

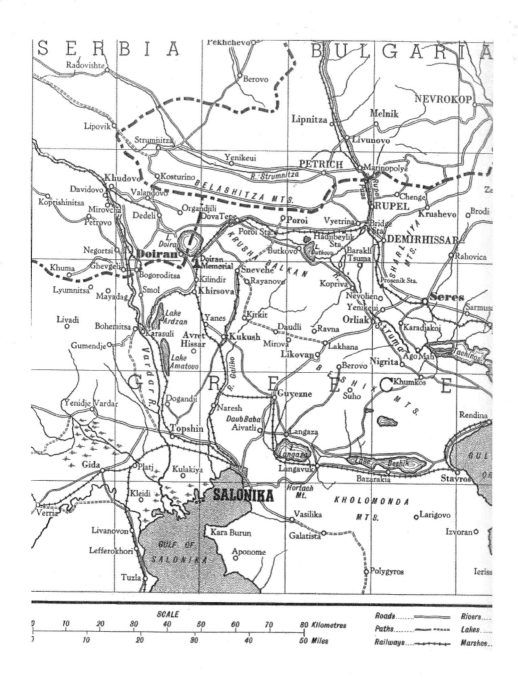

Map of Salonika c 1918
(Swinton collection)

The Great War

Young, fit men (and it usually is men rather than women) are driven by politics, passion, belief, fervour, and inspiring leaders to fight, kill or be killed in defence of their country. It is a fact of life and the consequences have to be lived with.

The reasons behind the start of the Great War, as it was known until 1939, were extremely complex, and it involved over 30 nations. Traditionally countries allied themselves to create a balance of power, and as a consequence when one nation was attacked, a domino effect came into play and the other countries were forced into a war scenario. The Great War followed this pattern and when Archduke Franz Ferdinand, the heir to the Austro-Hungarian throne was assassinated on 28 June 1914, the slippery slope to war was set in motion. During the next six weeks, some of the world's great powers formed two opposing alliances: the Allies (Britain, France and Russia) and the Central Powers (Germany, Austro-Hungary and the Ottoman Empire). On the 4th August, Britain declared war on the Central Powers.

Switzerland, Spain, the Netherlands, Scandinavia and Iceland retained neutrality in Europe but gradually many other of the world nations were drawn into the conflict e.g. Japan and America, and countries that were part of British, French, and Austro-Hungarian Empires also joined the war.

Soldiers at War

The British Expeditionary Force, made up of men from the regular army, soldiers on the reserve list and territorial soldiers, was sent to France in August 1914 and by the end of the year had been involved in the Battles of Mons, Le Cateau, Aisne and Ypres.   They had managed to halt the German advance through Belgium and France but at a terrible cost and the regular British army was virtually wiped out. The army numbers were boosted firstly by the Territorial Force which was expanded and then by volunteers who responded to Field Marshall Kitchener's 'Your army needs you' campaign.

Call to arms

On the outbreak of war in early August 1914, the newly appointed Secretary of State for War, Lord Kitchener appealed for 500,000 volunteers to join the armed forces. Right from the beginning of the war, there was great patriotic fervour in Britain and many hundreds of thousands of young men voluntarily turned up at recruitment offices to enlist often without telling their families until the deed was done.   The enthusiasm to join and fight was genuine, showing an "almost mystical patriotism". Sixth forms and universities, shops and offices, farms and factories were almost emptied as the war progressed.

Many men believed the war would be over by Christmas 1914 and saw this as an adventure and an opportunity to get away from everyday life and its mundane work. In 1915, a further 3.5 million volunteers were called for and as authorities realized that the war was not going to be over within months, many young men were determined to be part of the action, some even lying about their age at both ends of the scales.

There was a mass influx and on the 3rd September 1914 alone, over 33,000 men enlisted from every echelon of society. In the first month, over 115,000 miners answered the call and joined up causing major gaps in manpower in the North East pits. The numbers were much greater than Lord Kitchener imagined and this caused an administrative nightmare. Who would train, equip, feed and pay the recruits? The Times[1] gave examples that the peacetime army ordered 245,000 pass books, 250,000 service jackets and 43,000 greatcoats annually. In the autumn of 1914, the army ordered 6.5 million pairs of boots, 1.5 million greatcoats, 5.25 million service jackets, 11 million shirts, 5 million pairs of trousers, 4.5 million pairs of puttees plus socks, underwear, blankets etc. A further order was placed six months later. The industries that produced the clothes were being depleted as the men joined the army so women were quickly recruited to enable the orders to be fulfilled.

Conscription

Following the heavy losses at the Western Front, the government decided that compulsory military service was required to enable the country to have a strong fighting force. The Military Service Act was passed on 27 January 1916 and introduced conscription for every British male who on the 15 August 1915 was between the ages of 19 and 41, and who on the 2nd November 1915 was unmarried without dependent children. The first conscripted solders were accepted on the 2nd March 1916 and conscription continued until the end of the war. The act was extended to married men on 25th May 1916. The law went through several changes before the war's end with the age limit eventually being raised to 51. Provision was made for any man who had a preference to join the navy and the Admiralty had the first right of call on these men.

---

[1] Times Newspaper 7th November 1914

There were some automatic exemptions built in:

1. Men resident in Britain only for educational purposes
2. Existing regular or reserve forces who would be liable for foreign service but in the opinion of the Army Council are not fit for foreign service
3. Men serving in Navy or Royal Marines
4. Men in Holy Orders or regular ministers of any religious denomination
5. Men who had served with military or navy and discharged on grounds of ill-health or termination of service
6. Men who had been rejected for enlistment after 4 August 1914.

Application for exemption for a man could also be put before a Local Tribunal for the following reasons:

- if it was expedient in the national interests that he should be engaged in other work, or, if he was being educated or trained for any other work, that he should continue; or
- if serious hardship would ensue owing to his exceptional financial or business obligations or domestic position; or
- ill health or infirmity; or
- conscientious objection to the undertaking of combatant service.

If agreed, certificates of exemption would be issued, but if there was misrepresentation on the application, it could lead to imprisonment with hard labour for up to six months and this offence was not looked upon lightly. There were many stories about verbal and physical abuse of men who claimed exemption as conscientious objectors especially by families with men in the thick of the fighting or of those who had lost a loved one.

When conscripted, men were allocated into a Class, connected to the year of their birth and notified that they would be called-up in Class order. Class 1 was for those born in 1897 and therefore 18 years of age. They were told they would not be called-up until they were 19. Class 2 was for those born in 1896. Class 3 for 1895 and so on until Class 23 for those born in 1875. Notices were placed in prominent places advising the public on the date a particular Class would begin call up. In some cases individual notification was also given and individuals were expected to report for duty. According to the records found, the majority of the men from Witton le Wear were volunteers who enlisted prior to 1916.

Trench Warfare

Trench warfare on the Western Front started on the 12 September 1914 and continued until the last few weeks of the war in 1918. The trenches were the front line and very dangerous places, but behind were a mass of supply lines, communication trenches, training areas, stores, workshops, headquarters, kitchens, and ammunition supplies. Contrary to popular belief, the majority of troops were not in the front line at any one time, but in reserve, resting from battle, or supporting the infantry, artillerymen and the engineers, but they could all be called to the front to fight at any time.

The armies of 1914 initially fought a war of movement and trenches were dug for temporary cover only, but after the Battle of the Aisne in September 1914, both sides dug in to take cover and hold their ground. By November 1914, there were two continuous lines of trenches stretching over 400 miles from the North Sea to the Swiss border with 'no man's land' in between.

The majority of trenches around the Somme area were chalky and easily dug, and they were supported with wood, tin sheets and sandbags to prevent them caving in. The trenches around Ypres were built differently as the ground was very boggy and there was a high water table. These trenches were built up using earthworks, sandbags and wood. The trenches in France and Flanders ran through villages, industrial works, brickyards, across railway lines, through farms, fields and woods, over rivers and canals. Each area of trench presented its own challenges which had to be managed and overcome. The trenches followed the natural contours of the land and used natural features to enable a good defence or good view of the enemy. They often zig-zagged, which mean if a shell exploded in one of the sections, or if the enemy attacked, only that section was affected and could be defended. On many occasions the trenches of opposing sides were only 200 yards apart and the area between – 'no man's land' - became a killing ground lined with massive entanglements of barbed wire with metal pickets, wooden stakes and innumerable shell craters which all made attack difficult. Machine guns and artillery positions were established to offer protection to the troops in the trenches of both sides and manned constantly to fire at the enemy. Trenches including the supporting trenches were shelled and mortared frequently during the day ensuring that tensions never reduced. Men lived from hour to hour. Harry Patch a veteran of the WWI trenches said if you saw the sun rise, you did not know if you would see it set again. When in the front line trenches, the only time sleep was encouraged was between 12 midday and 4pm which was seen as the safest time of day. At all other times and especially during the hours of darkness, sleeping on duty was severely punished.

Gas attacks were also commonplace from the early days of the war. Poison gas was one of the most feared weapons of the war. Crude gas masks were given to soldiers but they had to be put on immediately gas was identified. Soldiers were also advised to use makeshift masks if they were caught in the open without a mask – urine soaked cloth would give protection against chlorine gas. Early gases used were designed to be more irritant than to kill, making victims unable to defend their positions. In 1915, chlorine gas was first used at the Second Battle of Ypres and when the allied soldiers saw the yellow cloud coming towards them, thinking it was a smoke screen, they were given orders to move the front line into the line of the gas. The effect of the chlorine was devastating and horrific for the allied soldiers and allowed the Germans to advance into the Ypres salient. Both sides then used gas as a major weapon of war but there were problems with its effectiveness as the gas was dependant on the wind to take it to the enemy. The wind was not always reliable and the poison gas often blew backwards over its own troops. Phosgene and mustard gases were devastating to internal organs and in many cases caused permanent blindness. Fatalities from gas attacks were relatively few (British Army had 188,000 gas casualties but only 8,000 fatalities) but the effects on the soldiers on both sides was terrifying. Many thousands of men survived the war but were so badly incapacitated by gas that they could not work when they returned to civilian life.

> Gas! GAS! Quick, boys! -- An ecstasy of fumbling,
> Fitting the clumsy helmets just in time;
> But someone still was yelling out and stumbling
> And flound'ring like a man in fire or lime . . .
> Dim, through the misty panes and thick green light,
> As under green sea, I saw him drowning.

'Dulce et Decorum est' by Wilfred Owen

The British Army did not like leaving soldiers too long with nothing to do. When not engaged in enemy action, the soldiers spent time training, carrying supplies, fixing and repairing damaged areas in the lines, and cleaning equipment which became part of a day's work, or night's work as most of the work was undertaken under the cover of darkness to protect the men from enemy snipers. Inactive soldiers were cold soldiers and working at night was a way to keep them warm and occupied leaving less time for 'thinking'.

The trenches also became the soldier's home. Underground dugouts were established and cavities were cut into the sides of trench walls, often with room for three or four men to shelter. The men slept, ate, washed and shaved, and performed all bodily functions in the trenches. Life back in Britain was not the centre of the soldier's lives and comrades became their families as they did not know what the next hour would bring. Life was very hard and for four years, soldiers lived and died here in every type of weather imaginable – snow, ice, fog, rain, wind and even some sunshine.

Fighting followed similar tactics on both sides. Heavy bombardment of the enemy trench with mortars and shells would be the signal that hostilities were starting. The aim was to destroy the artillery and communications networks in the opposing trenches, kill as many of the enemy as possible and destroy the wire defences and earthworks to allow the infantry soldiers to advance and take the enemies trench.

During the shelling, the troops in the trenches would shelter in dugouts or tunnels dug below the ground level and if lucky they would survive the bombing. This artillery bombardment could last for many hours or even days and then it would cease. Very shortly afterwards, the infantry would advance through 'no man's land' and close combat fighting often followed. Sometimes objectives would be captured and other times the advancing soldiers had to retreat in the face of enemy fire.

Recurrent artillery bombardment was also used to reduce the enemy's morale and keep tensions high by reducing the opportunities for the soldiers to sleep.

Christmas Truce 1914

The Christmas Truce of 1914 has been well recorded over the years and followed a period of unrelenting battles and hard physical labour to build the trenches. Both sides had been under the illusion that Christmas would see the end of the war. The soldiers were tired and were thinking about their families who would be celebrating Christmas without them. The truce was unofficial and not a planned occurrence - it just evolved as Christmas drew closer. During December, groups of German and British soldiers began to exchange seasonal greetings and songs were sung in both sets of trenches. At times, the tension was reduced to the point that individuals would walk across 'no man's land' to exchange gifts of food, cigarettes and souvenirs. This however, was not a total truce and sniping continued killing soldiers on both sides. The Officers on the front line were uncertain how to react and maintained a watching brief and did not issue orders to change the situation.

On 23rd December, a German soldier Karl Aldag[2] reported that German troops joining the line were bringing Christmas trees and candles and many were placed along the parapet of the trenches. On December 24th the weather changed from

[2] www.1914-1918.net

rain to hard frost which made life more bearable. Singing in the trenches became more evident keeping spirits high.

Christmas Day dawned, and behind the lines church services were held and where possible, Christmas dinners were eaten in barns and previously bombed buildings. In the front lines, some fraternisation with the enemy continued during the day when soldiers went out to 'no man's land' to find their injured comrades and collect bodies that lay there and arrange burials. There have been many strange events recorded when soldiers from both sides shook hands, exchanged tokens and in one area they even had a game of football. It is estimated that fraternisation with the enemy on Christmas Day 1914 took place in at least half of the British front. In other areas, the truce did not appear to happen and 81 British soldiers died on Christmas Day 1914, mainly victims of sniper fire. As night fell, things grew quiet and the soldiers went back to their respective trenches.

On Boxing Day, it started to snow, and officers and men resumed normal trench cautions. Senior officers, hearing of this unofficial truce were disturbed and General Sir Horace Smith-Dorrien, Commander of the British contingent issued strict orders forbidding friendly communication with the enemy and hostilities recommenced.

It is unlikely that any of the men from Witton le Wear were in the front lines at this time. The men who were enlisted prior to Christmas 1914, apart from Gerard Sadler who had been killed, were all serving and presumably training in the United Kingdom. They were Edward Hogg, Alec Richardson, Bertram Randall, Albert Brown, Fred Brown, Arthur Rutter, George Peacock, Jack Todd, Tom Bainbridge, and Joe Jackson.

Communication with home

When the soldiers were on active service, the families did not know where they were. Newspapers reported successful engagements with the enemy, but did not name regiments. Pre-printed field service postcards were given to the troops in the front line and soldiers could only score out the relevant sections, sign and date the card, but it did inform family that their soldier was still alive. Letters were the main source of information although they were heavily censored by platoon commanders to avoid sensitive intelligence information from being disclosed. Soldiers appealed for chocolate, home-made cake and treats and the families responded feeling that they were supporting 'their boys'. Occasionally other rank soldiers were issued with green envelopes in which they could place their letter and they signed the envelope to say it contained no sensitive information. This way they could exchange some private thoughts and feelings. A sample number were opened, but most of these letters escaped censorship.

Strangers were also encouraged to write to soldiers in an attempt to keep morale at the front line high. They also sent parcels with comforts such as knitted socks and blankets which were appreciated by the troops. In September 1915, the War Office established the Department General of Voluntary Organisations to co-ordinate the exchange of these parcels. It was reported that for every letter a soldier wrote, he received at least 4 in return. The timescale for delivery was 3 days to deliver letters to billets and 4 days to soldiers in the front line trenches. Every day in June 1915, the Army Postal Service handled 7,000 sacks containing ½ million letters and 60,000 parcels sent from the United Kingdom to servicemen overseas. In August 1916, the daily count had risen to 1.55 million letters and 110,000 parcels. 1.1 million of these letters were to the Western Front. There were also 37,000 free newspapers distributed to the troops during the month, to keep them in touch with domestic issues.

Children's contribution to Empire Day 1915

All school children were encouraged to bring a penny each to school on Empire Day - 20th May 1915. They had been given leaflets to take home explaining that the money raised would be spent to send parcels of chocolate, cigarettes and other comforts to the soldiers and sailors 'fighting the greatest fight for honour and freedom the world has ever known'. Every child who gave a penny received a certificate from the Overseas Club which promoted unity of British subjects throughout the world. This appeal was so successful it raised over 3 million pennies enabling over 250,000 parcels to be sent to the front line and was repeated in a Christmas Day Appeal later that year. The organisers were more ambitious with this second appeal as they stated:

"We hope every school boy and every school girl in Great Britain will give at least one penny. If you can spare two or three pennies it will be better still."

These were very successful appeals as each child was aware of someone whether in their own family or their friends' families or a neighbour who was fighting for the 'Empire' and it meant the children felt they were doing something special to help.

Home Leave

It is difficult to imagine how the soldiers felt when they went home following allocation of two weeks leave. It was an opportunity to escape from the squalor and the constant fear of the trenches. Each unit had two leave rosters, one for officers and one for the other ranks, which was strictly adhered to. Officers were allocated leave approximately every 20 weeks, but for other ranks it was often more than a year before leave was given. Compassionate leave was very rare, which maybe was the reason why Edward Hogg was so desperate to get home in April 1915 to see his new baby daughter. He was admitted to hospital with myalgia, vague muscle pain which was difficult to diagnose and easy to feign. His ploy did not work and he was returned to his unit.

Although only told a day or two before the leave pass was granted, soldiers could guess when their time was due and would be particularly edgy and nervous in the trench in case they were injured before they escaped on their allotted leave. Soldiers could not let their families know they were coming home until they arrived back in Britain. George Scott sent a telegram from Kings Cross Station on the 29th July 1918, the day he arrived in London telling his parents that he would be home in Witton le Wear later that night. What excitement this telegram would have started and no doubt there would have been great celebrations when their 'hero' returned.

Home leave was often wonderful in the soldier's imagination, but in reality it could be very difficult. Home and family would be much the same as it was pre-war but how strange this must have felt. It is difficult to imagine what it would be like – maybe like living in a parallel world with life going on, shopping, cooking, working, gossiping and no one being in fear of their life. Life in the trenches would feel like a nightmare and in many cases, the soldiers would not want to return. How could they tell their families what war was really like: the death, the destruction, the fears, the loss of comrades, and about the 'new family' that was waiting for their return to the trenches?   How traumatic it must have been for these young men, knowing they had to return to serve their country, and that they may never return to the bosom of their family. This was not the enthusiasm of their original enlistment - this was the reality of war that those who were left behind could never comprehend.   It is little wonder that after the war, returning soldiers rarely voiced their experiences.

Separation allowances and pensions

In 'The Times' of the 18th September 1914, the Prime Minister Herbert Asquith, declared that separation allowances paid to families of servicemen were to increase from 1st October 1914.

	Allowance per week	Decimal currency equivalent	Value in 2012
Wife only	12/6	63p	£25.20
Wife and 1 child	15/-	75p	£30.00
Additional child	2/6	13p	£5.20
Thus a wife with two children received £0.17s/6d per week (£35.20 per week in 2012 value).			

The husband in the armed services would contribute a maximum of 3/6d from his pay and the rest would be made up by the government.   It was estimated that the separation allowance would only cover about half a family's expenditure and this is the reason why so many women had to go out to work to supplement this meagre income.

Army pay offices which had 300 employees in peacetime, hurriedly recruited a further 3000 people in October 1914 to cope with the increased workload. These new recruits required training and this took time, hence some delays in payments to families which increased the hardship. The families of regular soldiers and those of territorial soldiers received their money fairly easily as the family status was up to date on the serviceman's records. New recruits also gave current information and payments were made quickly. The families of soldiers who were on the reserve list and recalled from civilian life, were not so lucky as the information about families had not been updated since they left active service which may have been up to six years previously. Many reservists had married and had children who were not recorded on the soldier's records. Notifications were placed in local newspapers informing wives how to claim allowances. Original birth and marriage certificates were sent into the army offices but often without details of the husband's regimental identity. This caused great delays of up to 12 weeks and severe hardship to families. This could have been what Jane Hogg experienced as she had two young children born in 1912 and 1913 when husband Edward, was recalled to the colours. This obvious chaos stopped many men from volunteering in the early days until they were sure their family would receive timely separation allowances. It is clear from the Witton le Wear soldier's records that the majority enlisted during 1915.

The Soldiers and Sailor's Families Association (SSAFA) had been formed in 1885 to support families left behind when soldiers went to war. In the first five months of the Great War,

SSAFA paid out over £1.28 million pounds to families in dire financial straits. They also gave support to families and Jane Hogg received such support when a SSAFA volunteer, Alice Lishman from Holly House, Witton le Wear helped her through the bureaucracy after her husband was killed.

In February 1917, the Ministry of Pensions was established to take over the responsibility for widows and disability pensions. The War Office had previously dealt with widows' pensions and the Royal Hospital of Chelsea had dealt with disability issues. Bringing them together seemed a sensible solution. Pensions along with separation allowances were not seen as a right and they could be withdrawn by the authorities at any time.

Separation allowances continued for a period of 26 weeks after the notification of the death of a soldier and for 30 weeks if the soldier was declared missing. At the end of this period, it was hoped that widow's pensions would have been arranged and in the case of the missing, there was a review of the case and further decisions made on what allowance would be paid. Widow's pension was calculated using the following variables – rank of the deceased, age of the widow and dependent children. The following table indicates the pension paid for a private's widow.

Year	Amount for a widow	Amount for 1st child	Additional children
1914 - 1915	7/6d	5/-	Incrementally decreasing per child
1915 - 1917	10/-	5/-	
1917 – 1918	13/9d	5/-	
1918	13/9d	6/8d	

It was estimated that the pension in 1918, was about two thirds of the family's pre-war income and it would automatically stop if the widow remarried.

Welcome Home Funds

Many villages established Welcome Home Funds from local donations, to show support to the returning soldiers after the war. Records about these funds are scarce, but in Witton le Wear money was raised by holding regular dances and whist drives in the school hall.[3] Money was also given from the fund to the families of soldiers killed. George Walton Scott's mother bought a clock in George's memory. What returning soldiers to Witton le Wear received is unknown, but some villages e.g. Blackhall and Ashington had medals struck, and some such as Newton Reigny in Cumberland and Middlesmoor in Yorkshire had certificates or illuminated addresses produced.

Other War Fronts

British and Allied armed forces including the Royal Navy also fought in Greece, Italy, the Middle East, Africa, the Mediterranean, North Sea, Atlantic and Pacific Oceans. In Europe the British and Allied naval forces were blockading the Central Powers to starve their supply of raw materials and food. Over the course of the war 5,399,563 men served with the Force, the maximum strength at any one time being 2,046,901 men.

Major Battles of the Western Front

The British Expeditionary Force on the Western Front grew from six divisions of British regular army and reserves in

---

[3] Auckland Chronicle throughout the war

1914, to encompass the entire British Empire's war effort in 1918.

Many battles were fought, the principle ones being:

1914	**1915**	**1916**
Battle of Mons	Battle of Neuve Chapelle	Battle of the Somme
Battle of Le Cateau	Second Battle of Ypres	Battle of Fromelles
First Battle of the Marne	Battle of Festubert	
First Battle of the Aisne	Battle of Loos	
Battle of La Bassée		
First Battle of Ypres		

1917	**1918**
Battle of Arras	Second Battle of the Somme
Battle of Messines	Battle of Lys
Battle of Passchendale	Second Battle of the Aisne
First Battle of Cambrai	Second battle of the Marne
	Hundred Days Offensive
	Battle of Amiens
	Battle of Ephey
	Second Battle of Cambrai
	Battle of Sambre

March – November 1918:   the final push by the German Army

The Central Powers agreed a peace treaty with Russia in March 1918 which allowed the Germans to concentrate their efforts on a major push at the Western Front. To break the stalemate, every possible German soldier and all the munitions that could be mustered were sent to the Western Front and on the 21st March, all hell broke out. During the next six months, 7 and possibly 8 of the 15 men (including A Smith) from Witton le Wear died in the most horrendous of circumstances. The war diaries from the 2nd Durham Light Infantry with whom John Sanders fought and died on the 21st March and the 1st Battalion

Kings Royal Rifle Corps with whom Frederick Hall lost his life on the 23rd March outline very clearly the horrors of that time.

The stagnation of the trenches changed to become a rapid advance and the Allies were pushed back 40 miles into France. Fortunately the Germans failed in two of their main objectives: to separate the British from the French troops and to capture the channel ports. On 18th July, the Allies finally broke the German lines, stopped the advance and started the last 'Hundred Days of the War'. The United States had declared war on Germany on April 6th 1917 and American troops joined the French and British in France and Flanders during the summer of 1918. They were fresh and not war weary and were invaluable in defeating the Germans which gave the allies an added boost. During August, September and October, the Allies forced the German army to retreat back into Germany.

There was also an increasing amount of unrest on the German home front, where the Allied blockade of the seaports was being felt. Sacrifices that were acceptable while the German armies were advancing were not tolerable now they were heading for defeat. 30th October was a key date as Turkey surrendered and the Austro-Hungarian Empire was collapsing. On 9th November, Kaiser Willhelm II of Germany, abdicated and went into exile in the Netherlands.

Armistice

At 11am on the 11th November 1918 the war formally ended. Rumours had been circulating the previous evening on the Western Front that the end was near. Orders to cease fire had been received in most cases and up to a few minutes before 11 o'clock, guns discharged, rapidly firing the remaining shells as a final salute. Van Emden (2011) records that Colonel Walter Nicholson of the 104th Army Brigade, Royal Field Artillery, wrote in the battalion's war diary that firing from the German lines was heavy all morning, including one particular wearisome enemy machine gun. Just before 11am, a thousand rounds were fired from the gun in a practically ceaseless burst. At 10.55am, the machine gunner got up, took off his hat, waved it at the British troops and walked away. No doubt he was thinking that he had survived this war and was going home.

Nobody is sure of the exact number of servicemen killed during the war but it can be approximated at:

Allies	Killed	Central Powers	Killed
Britain and Empire	958,000	Germany	1,800,000
France and colonies	1,400,000	Austro-Hungarian Empire	1,200,000
Russia	1,700,000	Turkey	325,000
Italy	650,000	Bulgaria	87,000
Romania	335,000		
USA	116,000		
Serbia	48,000		
Belgium	14,000		
Portugal	7,000		
Greece	5,000		
Japan	300		

Examples of four posters that were used to encourage the patriotic spirit in Great Britain.
(Author's collection)

Quiet time in the trenches. This is an example of a trench on the Western Front on a dry day. Note the three soldiers sleeping wherever they could find a space. Soldier on look-out keeping well below the parapet.
(Author's collection)

NOTHING is to be written on this side except the date and signature of the sender. Sentences not required may be erased. If anything else is added the post card will be destroyed.

I am quite well.

I have been admitted into hospital
{ sick } and am going on well.
{ wounded } and hope to be discharged soon.

I am being sent down to the base.

I have received your { letter dated _____
{ telegram „ _____
{ parcel „ _____

Letter follows at first opportunity.

I have received no letter from you
{ lately.
{ for a long time.

Signature
only. } Edgar.

Date _____

[Postage must be prepaid on any letter or post card addressed to the sender of this card.]

Field postcard sent to family in USA from the front line on 19th July 1916.
(Author's collection)

Empire Day certificate given to William Scott, younger brother of
George for donating pennies at school to the war effort.
(Courtesy of Scott Family)

Example of literature given to school children by the Overseas Club.
(Courtesy of Scott Family)

Board School, Witton le Wear. The school the local children all attended for primary education and where penny funds would have been collected. (Author's collection)

The post arrives at the front line. The expression on the soldier's face says it all (Swinton Collection, Imperial War Museum)

1914: Timeline on the Western Front

28 June
Archduke Franz Ferdinand was assassinated in Sarajevo

28 July
Austria – Hungary declare war on Serbia and invades on the 29 July

1 August – 3 August
Germany in support of Austria, declares war on Russia who had supported Serbia
Germany declares war on France

4 August - 12 August
Germany invades neutral Belgium
Britain declares war on Germany
USA declares neutrality
Austria – Hungary declares war on Russia
Serbia declares war on Germany
Austria – Hungary invades Russia and Poland
Britain and France declare war on Austria – Hungary

23 August – 30 August
First major British battle of the war begins – Battle of Mons
Japan declares war on Germany

5 September
First Battle of the Marne halts German advance in France and starts the 'race to the sea.'

12 September
Battle of the Aisne marks the beginning of trench warfare

19 October
First Battle of Ypres

29 October – 5 November
Turkey joins Central Powers
Russia declares war on Turkey
Britain and France declare war on Turkey

1 November 1914

Captain Gerard Sadler is injured and taken prisoner. He died in captivity.

25 December
Unofficial Christmas truce declared by soldiers along the Western Front

Gerard Gloag Sadler

'Of all the lovely scenes I've been privileged to see,
Not one of them for beauty could half compare with thee;
There are some pretty places to me are far more dear,
But thou art most beautiful, sweet Witton le Wear'.

Gerard is the most senior officer on Witton le Wear war memorial and the first to die in the conflict. He was born at Preston on Tees in 1881, the fifth and youngest son of Sir Samuel Sadler, an eminent manufacturing chemist and his wife Lady Mercy Sadler. The 1891 census showed him as a pupil at Durham Bow School along with his older brother Basil.

In 1899, Gerard enlisted in the army and was awarded his commission on the 5th September 1900. He was posted to South Africa to fight in the Boer War, initially with the Dragoon Guards, then briefly as a newly promoted Lieutenant in the 4th Durham Light Infantry. He then transferred back to the 3rd Dragoon Guards. Gerard was involved in several periods of enemy action between February 1901 and March 1902 including at the Transvaal, Orange River Colony and Cape Colony. He received both the Queen's South Africa Medal of 1901[4] and the King's South Africa Medal[5] with 1901 and 1902 clasps. After the war he served at Ballincollig in Ireland and then transferred to the 2nd Dragoon Guards in Aldershot where he met and married his wife, Phoebe Roche in 1908. Gerard reached the rank of Captain by the time he retired from army service on the 8th February 1911 at the age of 30.

Phoebe and Gerard seemed to spend the next three years travelling and the records from ship's passenger lists show they

---

[4] The **Queen's South Africa Medal** was awarded to military personnel who served in the Boer War in South Africa between 11 October 1899 and 31 May 1902.

[5] The **King's South Africa Medal** was awarded to all troops who served in the Boer War in South Africa on or after 1 January 1902, and completed 18 months service before 1 June 1902.

travelled round the world. In March 1911, they sailed from London on the SS Mishima Main, then on the SS Makura, and finally on the SS Arcadian. They travelled first class and visited places such as Colombo, Singapore, Hong Kong, Kobi, Sydney, San Francisco, New York, and Bermuda. Gerard and Phoebe arrived back in Liverpool during the spring of 1914 and moved into 'Briardale', a large detached house in the western end of Witton le Wear. It was presumably rented or loaned to the couple as the title deeds for the house do not name the Sadler's as owners. Gerard's father, Sir Samuel Sadler as well as being an industrialist, owned collieries in County Durham including one at Etherley, three miles from Witton le Wear. Maybe Gerard's plans were to take over his father's mining interests following his father's death in 1911 hence his link to this area of County Durham.

When WWI was declared on the 4th August 1914, Gerard did not hesitate and as he was still registered as an officer in the Army Reserve, he presented himself for duty with the 3rd Dragoon Guards along with his older brother Hereward, who was also a serving officer. They were amongst the first soldiers to arrive in France as part of the British Expeditionary Force at the end of August and quickly moved to Ypres where there was heavy fighting. During WWI, this particular area was thought to be one of the most violent places on earth and saw numerous and very bloody battles over the four year period.

Unfortunately, Gerard's army records have not been discovered, but the regimental war diaries give a clear description of what happened. Opposing armies met and fought in the town of Ypres on 7th October and four days later, the Germans withdrew to the Passchendaele Ridge to the east of the town. Captain Gerard Sadler, Captain Hereward Sadler and the 3rd Dragoon Guards moved to the trenches in the Wytschatte – Messines area south of the town of Ypres.

On 29th October they were in the front line of the trenches, west of Oostaverne and were heavily shelled all day. In the evening they were given orders to move back to Wytschatte-Messines area at dusk as the German infantry and marching guns had attacked so forcibly that they had to retire. The night was spent digging and improving the trenches.

30th October began quietly but by 10am they were again being heavily shelled with shrapnel and heavy percussion shells. This lasted all day, but the night was quiet.

31st October arrived with heavy shelling first thing in the morning and this continued all day. Again in the evening all went quiet and at dusk a German band was heard in the distance playing their national anthem. All was quiet until midnight.

1st November at 12.30am the Germans were reporting to be massing for an attack and at 1am, they attacked in such numbers, the British were unable to keep them back with rifle fire. The Germans won possession of the allied front line trenches and the war diary reports that the squadron leaders from that area went missing from that time. Gerard was one of the squadron leaders in the front line trenches. It appears he went over the top of the trench along with his men of 'A' squadron, was seriously wounded and lay in a shell hole in 'no-man's land'.

D.J.I. Fitzgerald, the historian of the Irish Guards wrote:

'The patience and gratitude shown by wounded men is one of the few things worth being in battle to see. At all times the silent courage of maimed, battered, bleeding soldiers lying in the open, or if lucky, in some muddy ditch or shell hole, was a living monument to the strength of human will in the

depths of human misery. A man drained of blood gets very cold, there is not much a man with a shattered thigh can do for himself; a man whose chest has been torn to ribbons by shell splinters would like to be moved out of the barrage. But they did not say anything, they didn't ask for anything; they smiled painfully when the orderlies or comrades put a blanket over them, or gave them a drink of water and a cigarette, and just shut their eyes for a moment when a shell exploded particularly close.'

This stoicism appears to be the same in all wars and when we have not personally experienced such terror, we wonder where this silent courage comes from.

Later when the fighting subsided, the ambulance stretcher bearers went out into the battle site, and Gerard was found with two brother officers and some of their injured men. The officers insisted that the men were rescued first. When the stretcher bearers returned to the crater, the officers had disappeared having been captured by the Germans. It appears that Captain Gerard Sadler died from his wounds on the 1st November whilst in captivity.

Captain Hereward Sadler took command of the remains of 'A' squadron along with his own men. You can only imagine Hereward's emotions taking over his brother's company and not knowing what had happened to his younger sibling.

Phoebe was staying in Tenter Close, Husthwaite, York when she was notified by telegram that Gerard was missing and when Hereward returned on leave at the end of the year, he made extensive inquiries as to Gerard's fate. It was not until early February 1915, that they received confirmation from the Swiss Red Cross Committee in Geneva that Captain Gerard Gloag Sadler had died from his wounds on 1st November 1914. His body was never found and his name is remembered on the Menin Gate Memorial in Ypres. This is a spectacular memorial to the fallen with the names of 54,896 officers and men of

Commonwealth forces who died between August 1914 and 15th August 1917 on the Ypres Salient with no known graves.

Every evening at 8pm, the local fire service buglers present a salute by playing 'The Last Post' as a daily act of remembrance and have done so every evening since 1927 excluding the years of the Second World War when the Germans again occupied Ypres.

Over 90,000 British soldier's bodies were never found or identified and their names are recorded on various memorials. It would be a nice thought that Gerard's body was already buried in one of these graves which states "A British Officer of the Great War – Known unto God", but we will never know. It is also thought that the bodies of over 45,000 men remain undiscovered in the fields of France and Flanders.

Gerard's obituary was published in the Durham Advertiser on the 19th February 1915. His will was published in the Durham Advertiser on the 24th September 1915 and his unsettled property value was £10,410 2s. 10d. He left his household and personal effects to his wife and the residue of his property to her during her widowhood. As he had no children, his will decreed £4000 to George Young Sadler Blair, his nephew who was a Second Lieutenant with the Royal Field Artillery. George was also a casualty of the war and was killed on the 24th July 1915 at the age of 21, and buried at Pont De Nieppe Communal Cemetery, near Armentieres. The residue of Gerard's estate was divided equally between the children of his brothers, Hereward, Basil and Stanley Aubrey, his half-brother, Cecil James and the children of Percy Alexander Field Blair. Gerard was posthumously awarded a bar and clasp for the 1914 Star, the Victory Medal and the British Medal.

Gerard is remembered on the Witton le Wear memorial but also on a memorial in All Saints Church, Preston on Tees, erected by the family. This is a marble plaque with a raised crest and motto, regimental insignia and the insignia of Durham School, a helmet and sword. It reads:

"Dedicated to Captain Gerard Gloag Sadler, 3rd Dragoon Guards, attached to the Carabineers, 6th Dragoon Guards. Son of Sir Samuel Sadler and Lady Sadler of Eaglescliffe. Served in South African War 1901 – 1902. Died at Messines, Belgium 1914."

Interestingly Gerard's name also appears on the Malton War Memorial, in Lanchester, County Durham. Malton is another place where Sir Samuel Sadler owned a colliery. The war memorial was erected to the memory of the men who worked at the Malton works and placed in the village memorial hall. When the hall later changed use, it was moved to the gable end of the house at 1 Official's Terrace in Malton. In the early 1960s, the plaque was removed as an extension was added to the building. It was stored in the house owner's garage where it was uncovered 45 years later. The plaque was restored and has been erected on a plinth at the entrance to the village. Gerard's name is first on the memorial followed by his nephew George Young Sadler Blair. After them come the names of 20 employees of the Malton Works who perished.

The issue of which regiment Gerard was serving with at the time of his death may seem confusing. The plaque erected in Preston on Tees stated he was serving with the 3rd Dragoon Guards, attached to the 6th Dragoon Guards. His medal roll card says he was on the roll of the 6th Dragoon Guards but his medals were on the roll of the 3rd Dragoon Guards. Witton le

Wear War Memorial states he was serving with the 9th Lancers and the Malton War Memorial states 3rd Dragoon Guards. From all the records reviewed, the 3rd Dragoon Guards was the Battalion that Gerard latterly served and died with.

1915: Timeline on the Western Front

18 February
German begins unrestricted submarine blockade of Britain and Britain blockade
German ports (11 March)

10 March – 25 May
Battle of Neuve Chapelle
Second Battle of Ypres   - first use of poison gas
Allied forces land on Gallipoli Peninsula
Lusitania sunk by German torpedo with American citizens on board (7 May)
Italy declares war on Austria – Hungary

17 July 1915
Edward Hogg died of wounds at Boulogne, France

5 August
Germans capture Warsaw

6th September
Joe Jackson begins his dairy on the Western Front

25 September

Battle of Loos

19 December
Allies withdraw from Gallipoli in Turkey

Edward Hogg

'They sing of Loch Lomond, Kilarney's Lakes as well,
But if they saw thy beauty, o'er them thou wouldst cast a spell;
And though thou hast no promenade, nor golden sands or pier,
No seaside village can compare with Witton le Wear.'

Edward Hogg was born in Richmond in June 1876, the youngest of six children and by the first decade of 1900, he was working as a limestone quarrier and miner in Weardale. He married Jane Dennison on 21st November 1908 in the Wesleyan Chapel in Wolsingham although they were both resident at Front Street, Stanhope. By 1911, they were living in Bridge End, Frosterley[6] and Jane had one child who had died in infancy. Edward was working as a quarryman and they later moved to Cemetery Bank in Witton le Wear and had 3 children, Kenneth born in 1912, Wilfred born in 1913 and Mary was born in 1915.

Edward was called up immediately war was declared as he was on the army reserve list under the category of Special Reservist. This was similar to the Territorial Army and in peacetime, men could enlist into the Special Reserve for 6 years and had to accept the possibility of being called up in the event of a general mobilisation. Their period as a Special Reservist started with six months full-time training (paid the same as a regular soldier) and they had 3-4 weeks training per year thereafter. A man who had not served as a regular soldier could extend his Special Reservist service by up to four years but could not serve beyond the age of 40. Edward was 38 years and 2 months when he attested on the 8th August 1914. He had most probably previously served with the 3rd (Reserve)

---

[6] 1911 England census

Battalion of the Durham Light Infantry whose job it was to provide reinforcement drafts for the active service battalions.

Edward's army records are very faded and difficult to read, so much so, that they have not been included in the www.ancestry.co.uk database. It took a specific visit to the National Archives at Kew to view his personal records. Edward was 5 feet 8 inches tall, weighed 138 lbs. and his chest measurement was 36 inches. His eyesight was perfect and he had blue eyes and light brown hair. His regimental number was 9891 and he was on home service in the United Kingdom during 1914 probably undergoing training for front line action.

On 26th January 1915, Edward sailed from Southampton with the 2nd Durham Light Infantry to join the British Expeditionary Force in France, leaving Jane who was heavily pregnant with their daughter and their two children living in Witton le Wear.

Edward was serving in northern France near Boulogne when on the 21 March 1915, his daughter Mary was born. Jane sent Mary's birth certificate to the Regimental Paymaster in York and her family separation allowance was increased within a week of the birth. There was no paternity leave in times of war and on the 16th April, Edward was admitted to hospital in France with myalgia, a form of muscle pain. Did he hope to get sent back to home to see his new baby daughter? If this was a ploy, it did not work as on the 24th April, Edward returned to his unit (2nd DLI, 18th Infantry Brigade, 6th Division) near Poperinge, west of Ypres and was very quickly back in the front line trenches.

The war diary for July 1915 of the 2nd DLI indicated they were in the front line for much of the time and when back in the reserve trenches resting, 5 Officers and 660 men were inoculated against typhoid. There is no mention of Private Hogg being wounded specifically on the 17 July, but during the month the casualties of the battalion were 1 Officer killed, 2 Officers wounded, 8 Other Ranks killed and 47 Other Ranks wounded, one of which was Edward. It is most likely that he was wounded with a gunshot wound to his head on the 11th July and transferred to the Field Casualty Clearing Station and then onto the 13th General Hospital at Boulogne. His condition deteriorated and on the 17th July Edward died and was buried in Boulogne Eastern Cemetery after serving 344 days in the army service.

The army information machine was quick and very effective. The Infantry HQ in York received a telegram on the 17th July at 10.29pm. It read:

C2 CaS p487 6 - 13 General Hospital Boulogne reports 9891 Hogg, 2nd Durham LI, dangerously ill. GSW head. Inform relatives. Proelicas.

Jane was informed and in Edward's army records is a letter from Alice Lishman of Soldiers, Sailors and Airman's Families Association (SSAFA) written on behalf of Mrs Hogg.

Witton le Wear
Co Durham
July 19 1915
Sir,

Mrs Hogg has received your notice that her husband No 3/9891 Private Edward Hogg, 2nd Durham Light Infantry is dangerously ill at 13 General Hospital, Boulogne. I would be much obliged if you can find out, and let us know if there is any chance of an improvement, or a chance of him being moved to a hospital in England as she would like to see him if possible.

I am
Yours Truly
Mrs Alice Lishman
Soldiers, Sailors and Airman's Families Association
For Mrs Hogg.

On the 18th July, Infantry Headquarters received a further telegram to say that Private Hogg had died and to inform his relatives. This letter will have overlapped with the news of Edward's death and Jane would have been notified on the 19th July after the previous letter had been posted. On 20th July, Mrs Lishman wrote a further letter on behalf of Jane.

Witton le Wear
Co Durham
July 20 1915

Sir,
I enclose Army Form filled up to claim for pension together with Mrs Hogg's marriage certificate and birth certificates of her children, all of which please return to her and oblige.

Yours Truly
Mrs Alice Lishman
Soldiers, Sailors and Airman's Families Association

This letter was received in York on the 21st July. Later that day, a local magistrate authenticated the certificates which were sent back to headquarters on the 23rd July and it was agreed that there would be the award of a widow's pension of 23 shillings to be paid weekly from the 24th July. Jane was notified immediately. This meant that from the time of Edward's death to the family receiving notification of the pension was 7 days. This payment would continue unless she remarried and for her children until they reached 16 years of age. It must be remembered that there was no state benefits or welfare state so immediate payment was essential to allow families to survive.

On the 4th December 1915 Edward's effects were sent to his wife with yet another army form. On the 29th July 1919, Jane was sent a letter informing her that '1914/15 Star' 'British

War Medal' and 'Victory Medal' was due to Edward and a memorial plaque would be sent to her. She received them on the 14th May 1920 when she and the children were living back in Front Street, Stanhope amongst her extended family. Edward's name was inscribed on the Witton le Wear War Memorial.

Captain Gerard G Sadler
(Author's collection)

Gerard Sadler's birth certificate 1881
(Crown Copyright - Author's collection)

Menin Gate Memorial
in Ypres – a memorial to
54,896 officers and men of
Commonwealth Forces who
have no known grave who
died between August 1914
and August 1917 on the
Ypres Salient.
(Author's collection)

Captain Sadler's name as it appears on
the Menin Gate Memorial
(Panel 3)
(Author's collection)

Memorial Stone at Malton Village, Lanchester erected by the Sadler
Family. Gerard Sadler and his much loved nephew George Blair are the
first names on the plaque.
(Author's collection)

Postcard of West End, Witton le Wear. Briardale, home of Gerard and
Phoebe Sadler can be seen on the left above the terrace houses.
(Author's collection)

Injured soldiers at a field clearing station on the Menin Road leading
from Ypres.
(Author's collection)

1908. Marriage solemnized at *the Wesleyan Chapel Wolsingham* in the District of *Weardale* in the County of *Durham*

No.	When Married.	Name and Surname.	Age.	Condition.	Rank or Profession.	Residence at the time of Marriage.	Father's Name and Surname.	Rank or Profession of Father.
80	Twenty first November 1908	Edward Hogg	33 years	Bachelor	Limestone Quarrier	Front Street Frosterley Stanhope	Robert Hogg	Roadman
		Jane Ann Dennison	29 years	Spinster		Front Street Frosterley Stanhope	Thomas Dennison	Limestone Quarrier

Married in the *Wesleyan Chapel* according to the Rites and Ceremonies of the *Wesleyan Methodists* by *Certificate* by me,

This Marriage was solemnized between us, *Edward Hogg* / *J A Dennison* in the Presence of us, *John Dobson Dennison* / *Herbert Dennison* — *Geo Southall Minister* / *Jn Geo Bainbridge Registrar*

Edwards Hogg's marriage certificate from 21st November 1908. The marriage took place at Wolsingham Wesleyan Chapel.
(Crown Copyright - Author's collection)

An example of and embroidered card made in France for soldiers to send home.
(Author's collection)

Swanking in uniform. Army Cyclist Corp possibly taken at Seaford, Sussex before embarkation to France in September 1915. Joe Jackson is third from the right and the uniforms look pristine.
(Courtesy of the Jackson Family)

Joe Jackson and a comrade in a Scottish Regiment during active service in France or Salonika
(Courtesy of the Jackson Family)

German Taube aircraft in a dogfight, as seen by Joe Jackson over Salonika.
(Fiddlersgreen.net)

Joe Jackson
in Washington, America
(Courtesy of the Jackson
Family)

Joe Jackson's account of life on the Western Front

Joseph William Jackson was born on 17th June 1894 in Witton le Wear. He was the eighth of ten siblings of Anthony and Mary Ann Jackson who lived at Sunny Bank, 9 Railway Terrace. In the 1911 census, his elder sisters, Elizabeth, Daisy May and Florence (Floss) had left home, but Edith, Barbara and Dora and brothers, Anthony, Thomas and Alexander remained at home. Joe was 16 years of age and working as a hardware warehouse boy.

Joe along with friends from Witton le Wear, Albert and Fred Brown, Arthur Rutter, George Peacock, Jack Todd, and Tom Bainbridge was one of Kitchener's men who answered the call that was made for young men to enlist with hope of ending the war by Christmas 1914. They all joined the 9th Border Regiment and Joe was transferred to the Army Cyclist Corps. His brother Anthony, a school teacher in 1911, enlisted at a later date and served with the 3rd Coldstream Guards and younger brother Thomas served with the 18th Yorkshire Regiment from 1918 on home service.

Joe wrote a journal from September 1915 through to August 1916 and this remains a family archive. The diary gives an impression of what was going on in the mind of young soldiers and how army life moulded their future lives.

Joe survived the Great War and was demobilised to the Army Reserve on the 18th February 1919 to be a coal hewer in the mines. In January 1920, he decided mining was not the way he wanted to live his life and emigrated to America on the USS Cedric. Joe went to Bruning in Nebraska where there were already other members of his extended family living and working as farmers. On 15th September 1920 he married his first cousin, Myrtle Ollie Jackson and they later had two sons,

Joseph Anthony Jackson, born on 1 December 1921 and Robert William Jackson born 12 July 1925. In 1926 Joe became an American citizen. He survived America's terrible depression in the "hungry thirties" and in 1937 he took his family to Kennewick, Washington looking for work and a better life. He died on 23rd March 1978 at the age of 83. There are now four grandchildren, seven great grandchildren and eight great great grandchildren living in the USA.

Joe began his army life in B Company of the 9th Border Regiment and in October 1914 he was serving at Seaford in Sussex. He received a post card with a photograph of St Philip and St James Parish Church in Witton le Wear from his friend E Ridley. In this card there is a sentence

"I can imagine how you will swank when you get your uniforms. You ought to be photographed."

These sentences relay the upbeat mood of the country at the time. Joe left for France as part of the Army Cyclist Corps in September 1915.

The following are extracts from Joe's diary.

Monday 6th September 1915
Arrived Amiens at 10 am, after travelling all night. Cycled to Flesselles. Terribly hot, Completely flagged out. Got into billets at last ..... barns with straw to sleep on, and rats galore for sleeping companions. Scorching hot during the day and freezing cold at night.

Tuesday 7th
Completion of first year in the army. Wrote home. Had a run around the country-side with cycle. Heard the guns for the first time. Picked apples from road-sides. Real beauties. Nearly every other tree was an apple or pear tree.

Wednesday 8th

Got up early. About 6am. Went for a long route ride. Sun got very hot towards midday. All of us very exhausted. Lots fell out on road-side. At last I gave up trying to keep up to the others. A few of us called at a Frenchman's house for water. Frenchie gave us wine instead. Greatly refreshed us. Set off on our way rejoicing and got back to billets only a minute or two after the others. Absolutely done up. Collapsed on straw and slept for 10 hours.

Thursday 9th

Went for a short walk and practiced map reading. In afternoon went for a ride. Saw many Indian Troops. Surprised to find how they respected us, greeting us with profuse 'sallams,' and addressing us as 'Sahibs.' Rations now consisted of bacon (breakfast) corned beef or Maconochie Rations (dinner), jam and cheese and biscuits (tea).

Maconochie Rations was a stew of sliced turnips and carrots in a thin soup produced by the Maconochie Company of Aberdeen. It was widely used as a food ration during the Boer War and WWI. Many soldiers came to detest it although it was readily eaten when famished.

Friday 10th

Got paid 5 Francs (4s./2d). Bought French Cigs. Rotten things. Like smoking 'twist'. On guard at night patrolling parts of streets. Every hour, each sentry would call out "all's well" to his 'next door neighbour' sentry who in turn would pass it on. The town clock would give the hourly chime and immediately after, the sentry's would call to the accompaniment of countless owls and barking dogs, disturbed from their dozings, while in the distance, the rumble of the guns continuously growling. Reminded of stories I had read, but never expected to be in actuality.

Saturday 11th

Came off guard at 7am. Put on a fatigue-party in afternoon. Worked the 'dodger' alright.

Joe often refers to 'the dodger' and it is thought that it means avoiding the duty if at all possible.

Sunday 12th

First Sunday in France. No Church Parade. Worked all morning. In afternoon, while off duty went for a quiet walk in the fields. Reading old letters and looking at photos of home. Homesick. Got bacca issued to us. Wrote home again asking for cigs.

Monday 13th

Had a long chat with Frenchman. He, - broken English and French, I, - broken French and English. Got a job on Div. H.Q. as dispatch orderly. Took a dispatch 8 miles. Got lost. Arrived back an hour late.

Tuesday 15th

Quiet day. Had a walk with French girl, or rather, she walked with me. (Isabelle) She, greatly amused at my attempts to 'parle Francais'. Quite enlivened me up.

Wednesday 15th

Very quiet. Took a few dispatches. Wrote home.

Thursday 16th

Very hard day. Got lost 15 miles from H.Q. Sun boiling hot. Rode at top speed. Got back at appointed time with dispatches. Wringing wet with sweat. Got parcel from home.

Friday 17th
Got paid 5 francs. Carried 9 dispatches roughly 65 miles all told. Dog tired and hungry. Only biscuits and bully to eat.

Saturday 18th
Left Flesselles. Went to Hangard. Very long hard journey. Nearer frontline. Saw star shells for the first time in the distance. Could hardly sleep for guns thundering. Bivouac in field at night.

Sunday 19th
Woke up frozen. Breakfast 6am. Went out signalling. Bivouac again at night. Another freezer.

Monday 20th
Started drilling in field. Disgusted at thought of 'forming fours' on active service. Left Hangard at 5pm. Arrived Proyart 11pm. Within 3000 yards of enemy trenches. Roar of guns terrible. Billets again. Straw for beds.

Tuesday 21st
Woke up with a start to hear shells screaming overhead. Thought my last hour had come. Got up and saw an aeroplane duel. Shelling other planes. Most exciting. Had a walk round the town. (Proyart was 29 kilometres from Amien) Most part in ruins. Saw a lot of German graves. Saw firing line in the distance.

Wednesday 22nd
Went out signalling, Flags attracted enemies fire. Had to run for it. Saw another aeroplane being shelled. Brought down in German lines.

Thursday 23rd

Village shelled for a short time. Exciting time. Started being one of orderlies for Cyclist Coy. Wrote home.

Friday 24th
Left Hangard for another place. Farther away from firing line. Billetted again. Not so good as last time, but still an interesting place.

Saturday 25th
Paid 5 francs. Got my watch by post. Wrote three letters.

Sunday 26th
Church parade. Name of place Harbonierres. Quite a fine town. Names of surrounding places. Guillacourt, Vignacourt, Bertangles, Albert, Villers, Brettoneaux, Bray, Wrote two letters home. Got 20 cigs from Company.

Monday 27th
Morning – nothing important. Afternoon – saw many air duels. Clear hot day.

Tuesday 28th
Went out signalling in morning. Shifted our billet. Better one. Bob Clarke had his nose burst by rifle falling off peg onto his face while asleep. Most amusing to us, but rather hard on him.

Wednesday 29th
Quiet day. Nothing doing.

Thursday 30th
Hard day. Carried dispatches nearly 80 miles. Dead beat.

Friday 1st October
Paid 10 francs. Happy again. Carrying dispatches till midnight. Got a few frights on the road. District around

here is renowned for its alarming numbers of pro-Germans. Wasn't quite safe to be alone at night. My last return journey was made in black-darkness. Orders not to light lamp. Coming down a steep hill. Road greasy and dangerous. Suddenly heard a call, "Halte, Qui va la?" Could just make out a bayonet shimmering about 10 yards ahead. Daren't apply brakes. It would have meant a bad smack. Suddenly remembered French reply and called out "Amie, Anglais." Sentry snatched back his bayonet and I slithered past with my heart in my mouth. Got off my bike at bottom of the hill shaking like a leaf. That bayonet was within 3 feet off my chest when he snatched it back. Walked the remainder of journey (about 1½ miles).

Sunday 10th

No Church Parade. Off duty all morning. Air duel in afternoon. Neither side won.

Monday 11th

Quite pleasant day. Nothing important.

Tuesday 12th – Friday 22nd

Very quiet time. Almost forgot there was a war on. Got to know many of the French folk. Had the embarrassing 'pleasure' of being embraced by old dame at one house. Wouldn't have minded if she had been of my own age.

Joe and his company had spent six weeks in the Western Front and was then ordered to pack up again. It took a week to travel by bicycle, lorry, train and foot to Marseilles where they march through the streets on the 30th October. They had a great reception from the townsfolk even although it was 1am and boarded the troopship S.S. Egra at 2.30am. Joe then discovered that the Border Regiment were on board and he was greatly joyed to know he would sail with his friends, Jack Todd, George Peacock and Albert Brown before settling into a well-deserved sleep. The ship left Marseilles for Alexandria at daybreak on the 31st October and Joe found Jack, George and Albert.

This was a very pleasant time for the lads. Deck sports were organised and Joe won first prize in the obstacle race and concerts were held at night. During the hours of darkness, there were no lights or smoking allowed on decks because of the risk of submarine attack. Everyone had to wear lifebelts at all times and men were constantly standing by the lifeboats to lower at a moment's notice. When they arrived at Alexandria and anchored, the four Witton le Wear men dived overboard and spent a good deal of time enjoying the warm water. Rafts were lowered with men who could not swim so they could enjoy the water as well. Two days later the ship sailed on through the rich, deep blue Aegean Sea, weaving through submarine infested waters to reach Salonika in Northern Greece on the 8th November.

Bulgaria had sided with the Central Powers and attacked Serbia which was an ally of Britain, France and Russia in October 1915. The Greeks had asked for military assistance from Britain and France to help them maintain their treaty with Serbia. Joe and his comrades were part of the small force sent to this area. The British contingent advanced to the front line in Macedonia but was too late to support the Serbs who retreated into the Albanian mountains. The Allies withdrew back to Salonika, set up an entrenchment camp known colloquially as the 'birdcage' and waited for the Bulgarians to attack.

As the S.S. Egra approached the harbour, the guns of the fort fired at them. The soldiers later found the Greeks were firing blanks as they were celebrating the fourth anniversary of their freedom from the Turks. Joe said his farewells to Jack, George and Albert and left Salonika with his company riding their bicycles. As soon as they left the town, they found the roads were ankle deep in mud and they had to stop every few yards to clear their mudguards and spokes. All the road traffic was mules, donkeys and oxen and after a hard day, they bivouacked about 7 miles from the city for the night. Their only food was bully beef, biscuits and a little jam.

Thunderstorms, snakes, jackals, wild dogs, lizards, scorpions and mosquitoes were numerous. On 12th November Joe received his first mail from home for over a month and was in good spirits. On the 25th November another mail delivery arrived but three mailbags had gone missing and Joe was down-hearted. In the last mail bag Joe received four letters and a parcel from his sisters Floss and Edith and he was again happy.

Joe became an expert flag signaller and used lamps at night. When not doing this he was assigned to general duties. Over the next two weeks the weather deteriorated, snow blizzarded and it became very cold. There were twelve men in Joe's tent and they slept huddled together in two's and three's to try to stay warm. They wore everything they could find, mufflers, gloves, overcoats, blankets and sacks. At night, the sentry would come round to waken everyone every hour to ensure they could get up and walk around to keep from freezing. All the traffic came to a standstill and they still only had the same rations as previous. It was a miserable time for the soldiers but they still had duties to perform and signalling was needed on the outposts at night to keep order. Joe noted in his diary that it was not safe to go out even as little as 100 yards, as the Greeks had a treacherous disposition and were all around the camps. Arms were carried at all times and the men never went out alone.

Early December was better. Weather was improving although the snow remained, but it was less cold. Joe received a parcel from his sister Dora with socks and on the 4th he was given bread – a 1lb. loaf per day for each man. On the first day, Joe's bread was eaten for breakfast – a feast for a king.

Although there was fighting on the front line further north, there was little work for cyclists and signallers to do at this time. Joe wrote that they all wished they could go up to the front line for some action as it was getting lonely back near Salonika.

Friday 15th December

About 150 of us went down to Salonika docks to unload a large cargo boat. Pouring with rain. Drenched through in no time. Couldn't get to work right away. Bummed around the docks nearly all day 'pinching' tins of jam and milk and dates from piles of rations on the dockside. 'Pinching' or 'winning' something was the polite way of speaking when it meant stealing, that word being too coarse or vulgar for such honest persons as we. We only 'pinched' when we knew we were hurting no one but the army authorities and the Greeks. Those scoundrels pinched off us, so we pinched back.

Started working on the boat at 6pm. Worked till 12pm. We 'manned' the whole ship from men in our regiment who had been sea-faring men in civilian life. Still wringing wet. Water oozing out of my shoes. No tobacco, no cigarettes, no money – absolutely miserable.

Slept on the largest tramp steamer afloat for four hours. Started working again at 4.30am. Kept taking turn and turn about working in the ship's hold for an hour or two and then working on the quayside in the rain. Got relieved by another regiment at 10am. Not raining now but still wet through. Had a blanket each to carry back and we rolled them up and put them over our shoulders in bandolier fashion. Inside the roll of blankets we hid our tins of jam and milk. We also had them stuffed up our coats. Had to pass the guard of the dock in coming away. Was plumb scared in case they would discover the tins. Sometimes one would fall out clattering into the gutter, with the man who owned it trying to catch it as quickly as possible. However we got safely back to camp with our ill-gotten gains. In our tent of 8 men we had altogether 14 tins of jam, 8 tins of milk, and 3 Maconochie Rations. To cap it all we were complimented by the General for doing such good work.

---

9 Sunny Bank, Witton le Wear, 2nd Dec. 1915

My dear Joe,

This is to let you know that we have posted with the same post as this, one well sewn up parcel and if it doesn't reach you in safety, I'll eat my shirt? Beg pardon. Thought you would like this photo of your old bathing place. It is a good one is'nt it? Have you any idea where Arthur Rutter is? His mother has not had any word from him for quite a while. I think he left France about a fortnight after you boys did. They asked if we would mention it to you and Jack. Well Joe, I'll wish you the best of luck. Love from everybody. Yours lovingly Dora

---

At home in Witton le Wear, Dora wrote a postcard with a picture of the bridge over the River Wear and posted it to her brother on the 2nd December.

Arthur Rutter was another of the Witton lads who enlisted in 1914. Joe received this card on the 21st December and the parcel on the 24th December along with another letter and two other parcels from Floss and Mrs Lishman. This is the same Alice Lishman who lived in Holly House, Witton le Wear and volunteered with the Soldiers, Sailors, and Airman Families Association (SSAFA) that supported Jane Hogg. Evidently she sent Christmas parcels to all the servicemen from Witton le Wear which were very welcome. On another date, Joe also received a letter from Mr Tymms who was the headmaster of Witton le Wear Board School so the men who were fighting for their country were not forgotten in the village.

Joe's diary for Christmas is transcribed below.

Friday 24th
Nearly went over the moon for joy – 10 parcels in our tent altogether. Couldn't get all the stuff stowed away. Had the best meal we have had for months. Shared our parcels among us all, to make them last longer. Got choir together after supper and sang old songs and Xmas carols. 5 bases, 3 tenors and 10 trebles. Quite a lively time. Spent a good old fashioned Xmas Eve. No 'lights out' at night. Lay in bed relating our separate stories of old Xmas's gone by. Quite surprised and delighted to find so many stories very much like my own. Fell asleep about midnight, dreaming of a nice warm fire-side at home, with all the good cheer mixed up with rifles and bombs and guards and fatigues.

Saturday 25th Xmas Day
No parades. Good breakfast. Boiled my Xmas pudding about 11.30am. Got rum served out and I saved mine for

my Xmas pudding. Roast beef and potatoes for dinner. Ate my pudding with rum and sugar. Real fine. I can still taste it. Wonder what they are all doing at home. In the afternoon had a bath in a warm stream in the hillsides. Played football till tea-time. Good tea. Toast, butter and jam and finished off with Xmas cake. Had another good sing-song at night.

This was how Joe spent the end of 1915 in Greece. When not working he was bored and wanted to see some action. He was wet, cold, and intermittently worked hard in conditions that varied between snow, ice and freezing temperatures and when the weather warmed up a little, everything became caked in mud. It was not a pleasant experience.

1916: Timeline on the Western Front

January – August
Joe Jackson served in Macedonia

21 February – 31 August
Battle of Verdun commenced and became the longest battle of the war between the French and the German armies.

31 May – 1 June
Battle of Jutland – the largest naval battle in history

1 July – 18 November
Battle of the Somme began and ended with over 60,000 British casualties on the first day – the heaviest loss is a single day since the Battle of Waterloo in 1815.

15 July
Lieutenant Henry Maguire killed at Mametz Wood

28 July
Private Alec Richardson killed at Fosse

15 September
Tanks first used by British forces

25 September
Private William Allinson died near Gueudecourt

Joe Jackson and the Gardeners of Salonika

The Allied soldiers fighting in Greece became known in Britain as the 'Gardeners of Salonika' due to the fact that they were ordered to grow vegetables to supplement their rations. In the UK, the war in Salonika was seen as an easy posting but as Joe and his comrades found, this was not the case. Trenches were established in northern Greece where trench warfare and heavy fighting was experienced similar to that of the Western Front. As well as the extremes of weather conditions, malaria was endemic amongst the troops.

On the 7th January 1916, the Salonika area was bombed by German Taube fighter planes. Bombs landed within yards of Joe and four others who were working in a ploughed field. They found cover and watched the air duels which they found exciting and made them forget the danger they were in.

Blizzards continued through January and February and many times they could have cried with the cold. An example from the diary reads as follows:

Snow started freezing on us. Went with wagons 4 miles to help unload. One mule died on the road. Had to leave him at the side of the road. Other mules wouldn't face the blizzard. Put sacks around their heads and got them to go. Took us 2½ hours to go 4 miles. Had to walk back to camp afterwards in the teeth of the blizzard. Sometimes we hung to the back of the wagon and then our hands would get too cold to hold on and we would stumble through the snow as best we could. Back at the tent we had to clear the snow from our tent door and then get fires going. Sat in bed with little fires in old biscuit tins trying to dry clothes.

On Thursday 3rd February, Joe moved to a new camp 2½ miles from Salonika town and he was delighted when he met Arthur Rutter from Witton le Wear. They spent much time together over the next few months chatting about home and exchanging news. The weather improved and life continued very much as before.

Monday 27th March was a 'never to be forgotten day'. Joe was sleeping in a cemetery area between the grave stones and was rudely awakened by sudden horrific noise of bombs, guns, machine guns and the whir of aeroplane propellers. He quickly pulled on his clothes and saw three enemy aircraft overhead hunting for victims. Joe said he understood how a mouse felt when a hawk hovered overhead. Joe and Bob Clarke found an area of shelter dodging the shrapnel and fragments of high explosive which were falling all around the cemetery. More bombs fell, houses quaked and trembled, windows shattered, tombstones collapsed and it was like 'hell on earth'. Although concussed, Joe and Bob survived. The Germans had blown up the nearby French ammunition dump and the area around it was devastated. Joe and Bob tried to help some of the injured people but in many cases, their help was not enough. 30 Greek civilians and 12 Greek soldiers, 45 French soldiers and 1 British soldier were killed. 50 Greek civilians, 8 Greek soldiers, 47 French soldiers and 6 British soldiers were wounded.

That night Joe and his comrades could not sleep, the slightest noise made them jump, so they just sat and talked and smoked until their turn for sentry duty came round. Jim Marsden, another soldier picked up his mandolin and played quietly ♫ 'Keep the home fires burning'♫ which helped sooth the nerves and calm the tension.

At the end of April, Joe met up with Albert Brown and Arthur Rutter and they told Joe about the Zeppelin raid over Bishop Auckland on the night of 5/6th April. 23 bombs were dropped at Evenwood and Randolph Colliery and 27 bombs south east of Bishop Auckland. Many houses were damaged but there was only one fatality.

Joe continued his war in Salonika until his diary ends in August 1916 when they were ordered to move northwards further up the line. After much travelling they arrived at a valley near Lake Doiran and found his company. They sat on the hillside listening to the Band of the South Wales Borderers. War – what war!

Joe continued serving in the Army and was eventually demobilised along with his two brothers at the end of the war.

Henry Maguire

'Many spots of beauty, there are all along the dale,
That stretch from St John's Chapel down to Bedburn in the vale;
But should an artist pass this way his easel he would rear,
And choose thee from amongst them all, fair Witton le Wear.'

One name on the Witton le Wear War Memorial is Lieutenant H McGuire, Royal Engineers. According to Army records and the Commonwealth War Graves Commission there was no Lieutenant H McGuire with the Royal Engineers who died during WWI. There is however, a 2nd Lieutenant Henry (sometimes called Harry) Maguire of the Royal Engineers and he is the most likely candidate for 'our H. McGuire'. Ireland's memorial records show Henry was born in Belfast[7] and in 1911, Henry was living with his parents Henry and Mary at 24 Duncairn Gardens, Duncairn, County Antrim. Henry was a 27 year old civil engineer. The entry for his mother Mary shows she was either born in County Dublin or County Durham as the writing is unclear. By 1916, the family had moved to 16 Trevelyan Terrace, Belfast and his father died on the 18th March. Incorrect spelling of names, regiments and rank was common on memorials. Being an engineer could be a reason why Henry enlisted with the Royal Engineers, but without any army records being available, it is difficult to be certain.

There are no McGuire or Maguire families recorded in Witton le Wear in the 1891, 1901 or 1911 census, so the link to the village remains a mystery. There is evidence in the war diaries of Henry's regiment that he went on leave from France on the 22nd March 1916 when he proceeded to England and Ireland which links to his father's death. His mother was

---

[7] Ireland's memorial records 1914-1918, p.188

62

certainly in Northern Ireland in 1922, as his medals were sent, care of his mother to Downpatrick.

Somebody in the village must have requested Henry's name to be inscribed on the Witton le Wear War Memorial and this would also explain the possibility of the wrong spelling of Maguire if it was not a direct family name. According to the war memorial, Henry's regiment was the Royal Engineers which confirms this as our Henry Maguire.

Henry was awarded his commission with the Royal Engineers[8] on the 16th October 1915. He served in France at the No.4 General Base at Rouen, and then joined the 124th Field Company on the 10th March 1916[9] near Givenchy. As his army records have not survived, the following information is taken from various records including the CWGC, war diaries and medal rolls index.

The war diaries of the 124th Field Company from March to July 1916 give a fairly clear picture of what was happening to the sappers and officers. It appears they were in northern France and regularly moved about the area. Each move was identified in detail in the diary. In March, the company were cleaning out and draining trenches, timbering and enlarging dug-outs, rewiring, repairing, building new trenches and constructing machine gun emplacements around Fauquessart.

On the 12th April, 2nd Lieutenant Maguire returned to duty from leave in Ireland and England and went straight back into front line action. On the 22nd May, he was wounded and hospitalised but returned to duty on the 4th June near Basnes. Over the next month, the battalion marched over 150 miles through Auchel, Villiers Brulin, Ransert, Epicamps, Val de

[8] Army List November 1915
[9] Army List May 1916

Maison, Toutencourt, Berrincourt C'abbe, and by the 5th July, they were at Mametz Wood joining the 38th Welsh Division. The battle for Mametz Wood started on the 10th July and was a battle that saw bravery beyond imagination by the Engineers and the Welsh Division. The memorial erected on the site is that of a Welsh Dragon which marks the area where over 4,000 British troops became casualties of war over the three day battle.

Henry was involved in the fighting on the 10th July from 3am until 9pm when the battalion held a strong position at the crossroads. There was some respite overnight and then Henry was involved in strengthening the front line. There was further fighting the following day, and Henry and another officer were wounded along with 16 other ranks; 3 other ranks were killed and 5 other ranks were posted as missing.

Henry was treated on the battlefield and then taken to No 21 Casualty Clearing station at Corbie for further treatment but died on the 15th July. Henry was buried in La Neuville British Cemetery, Corbie, and was one of the first men buried in this new cemetery established to take the bodies of soldiers who died in the area of the River Somme.

The link between Henry and Witton le Wear is not resolved but hopefully in time more information may be disclosed to finally identify Henry's connection to the village.

Alexander Lister Richardson

'The exquisite delight I feel in words I can't explain,
As I look on thy splendour from the hill top in the lane;
If I could roam this island o'er, in this I am sincere,
Thy equal I would never find, sweet Witton le Wear.'

Alexander Lister Richardson is remembered on the grave of his parents in Witton le Wear Cemetery and also on the War Memorial in Wolsingham School. The gravestone reads:

'In loving memory of John, beloved husband of Mary Jane Richardson of Harperley Post Office who died March 4th 1907 aged 53 years also of the above Mary Jane Richardson who died September 3rd 1951 aged 89 years also Alexander Lister, their son who died in France 28th July 1916 aged 28 years. Thy will be done.'

The school recorded the name he was known by as Alec and he had been born in Wolsingham in 1889, the fifth of eight children. His father John was a railway plate layer and they all lived in a railway house at Harperley Station cottages, before moving to Harperley Post Office. Alec went to Wolsingham Grammar School from September 1905 until July 1907. He excelled at sport and became the captain of both the school football and cricket teams. Alec received the English Prize at the 1906 speech day and moved from Wolsingham Grammar School to Sunderland Training College where he was elected by his peers as prefect of the junior male students. In 1911[10] he was working as an assistant school master at elementary level and lived at 3 Prospect Terrace, Chester le Street with his widowed mother, his grandmother aged 83, two younger sisters and a brother.

Alec enlisted in the Durham Light Infantry in 1914 and his medal card stated he was awarded the 1914/15 Star, the Victory Medal, and the British Medal. The record also indicated

---

[10] 1911 census

that Alec served in Egypt. The 18th Battalion was the only service battalion of the DLI to serve in Egypt at this time so it is safe to assume that Alec served with 18th DLI. When reviewing the Absentee Voters List of October 1918, it is evident that Joseph Stobbs, from Witton le Wear was also serving alongside Alec at this time.

The battalion left Liverpool on the 7th December 1915 on the SS Empress of Britain. The voyage was uneventful until 13th December when sailing in the Mediterranean, the ship collided with a French ship cutting her almost in half. Two firemen were killed but everyone else was rescued and taken to Valetta Harbour in Malta where they stayed for three days for ship repairs before sailing on. The soldiers eventually disembarked at Port Said on the 22nd December. None of the extra rations expected were received in time for Christmas so ration packs were the food of the day. Ration packs were individual supplies of dried products, tins, biscuits, chocolate and drinks given to each man to last for a 24 hour period.

18th DLI's role was to keep the enemy well back from the shore to avoid shelling of allied ships. Digging trenches in loose shifting sand was a very tiring job and sandstorms kept filling them in as quickly as they were being dug. On the 2nd March, 1916, the battalion received orders to go to France. They had spent just over two months in Egypt during the best season of the year. Sea bathing, heavy marching, heavy digging and rather Spartan fare made the officers and men very fit and the time was reported in the battalion war diary as being interesting and enjoyable.

The battalion sailed to Marseilles, arriving on the 11th March 1916 and travelled on a train northwards, where the French authorities supplied rum and coffee to the troops. On reaching their destination station in northern France, the soldiers marched 12 miles through snow and freezing weather – what a change from the Egyptian sunshine. On the 25th March, Alec and Joseph were on the front line in waterlogged trenches.

On the 1st July 1916, Alec and Joseph survived the most disastrous day in British army history where there were 60,000 casualties. Their objective was a line running south east of Serre and the infantrymen gathered in the assembly trenches at 4.50am. The soldiers knew this was to be an important battle and the nerves and anxieties of the men in the last few hours before they went over the top are difficult to imagine. The British artillery had been firing a heavy barrage over the previous week to destroy the German front lines, dugouts and communications. At 7.20am mines were detonated under German trenches at Beaumont Hamel. At 7.30am the British soldiers with 30 kilograms of equipment, including shovels and wire cutters, climbed out of their trenches and marched as ordered, wave upon wave with bayonets fixed towards the German trenches.

Unfortunately the artillery siege of the previous week had failed to take out the enemy targets and the Germans were well prepared for the expected onslaught. In many areas of the Somme, allied soldiers were killed by their thousands in 'no man's land'. The 18th DLI war diary outlines hour by hour what occurred over the next four days they were in the front line trenches where there were heavy casualties in all sections. Trenches were blown out of existence, there was heavy enemy bombardment with explosive and tear gas shells, gas attacks were threatened and the war diary reports 11 officers and 289 other ranks from the 18th DLI were wounded or killed in the first two days of the battle. Alec and Joseph survived this horrendous time and late on the evening of the 4th July, the battalion were relieved from front line duties. Over the next three weeks they route marched via Louvencourt, Beauval, Berneuil, Conteville, Berguette, La Pierriere to Fosse.

At 8am on the 27th July, the 18th DLI were again in the front line and by 9.30pm they were feeling the effects of a full bombardment of German artillery followed by German raids. The bomb store was hit by shells but the fire was eventually extinguished. The communication trenches were also obliterated which caused major difficulties for the commanders of individual companies. 'B' and 'C' Companies were attacked at 1.30am and at 4am various bays of the trenches where 'C' Company were situated were blown up and a number of soldiers buried. Over 50 German soldiers attacked the trench line, but were repelled by the remaining allied troops. 'A' company was also attacked but firing from the Lewis gun stopped the enemy from reaching the trenches.

Alec was deeply involved in this battle, and he sustained fatal injuries during the night. He was taken to the field casualty clearing station where he died of his wounds later in the day. He was buried in one of the 103 small local burial grounds near the dressing station but later reburied at Cabaret Rouche British Cemetery in Souchez, near Arras where 7,655 World War I soldiers are buried, more than half unidentified.

In the grounds of Wolsingham Grammar School is a memorial oak planted by Alec's niece Beatrice Laidlow in 1918 when she was a first year pupil at the school and his name and photograph appear on the school memorial. Alec is also remembered on the war memorial in St Mary and St Cuthbert's Churchyard in Chester le Street, his home town during the war.

William Allinson

'The peasant stands a better chance to marry a princess,
Than I have of painting thy brilliant loveliness;
Thy Castle and thy Towers, the river flowing clear,
Are only some of thy great charms, dear Witton le Wear.'

William Allinson was born in Masham, North Yorkshire in January 1883. He had two brothers and two sisters and his father died around 1886. His mother worked as a laundress to keep the family fed and clothed. They moved to Liversedge near Wakefield to be closer to William's paternal grandparents around 1901 and by 1911, William's mother Jane, still working as a laundress, was living in Harrogate with her unmarried daughter Ada.

William had been working in 1901 as a collecting agent and travelled around the countryside. He met and married Caroline Sarah England in 1908. Caroline previously had an illegitimate daughter Margaret who was born in 1901. In 1911 they were living at High Bondgate in Bishop Auckland and had two further young sons, William and George. William's occupation was a self-employed mechanic, but he was later described as a watch and clock repairer.

In Bishop Auckland, William like many others joined the Durham Light Infantry Territorials and when war broke out he was transferred to the Kings Own Yorkshire Light Infantry on the 28th March 1915. He was shipped to France in September 1915. His first experience of war was horrifying as within a few days of active service and lengthy forced marches, he was fighting in the later stages of the Battle of Loos, where the Division suffered over 3,800 casualties with minimal gain.

In 1916, William again experienced the horrors of war near Mametz, during the first days of the Battle of the Somme and then in the middle of July he fought at Bazentin Ridge. There was a stalemate situation in the trenches until September, when there was the renewal of the offensive by the British Army. William was involved in fighting between Flers and Courcelette and on 25th September, they broke through the German lines on the Transloy Ridges in the Battle of Morval. The weather had suddenly turned autumnal and the battlefield was increasingly difficult stretching men to the limits of physical endurance. The 21st Division went onto capture the town of Gueudecourt but during enemy artillery shellfire attacks on the outskirts of the town on the 25th September, William was reported as missing, presumed killed in action.

Caroline did not receive official notification from the War Office of William's death until Thursday 2nd November 1916.[11] She had moved from Bishop Auckland to Wear Terrace, Witton le Wear with her five children, two having been born after 1911.

William is remembered on the massive memorial at Thiepval which commemorates 72,191 British and South African soldiers with no known graves who died in the Battles of the Somme between 1915 and 1918.

William is also remembered on the Witton le Wear War Memorial and Caroline later received William's British and Victory medals.

---

[11] Auckland Chronicle, 9th November 1916

CENSUS OF IRELAND, 1911.

Two Examples of the mode of filling up this Table are given on the other side.

FORM A.

No. on Form B. 24.

RETURN of the MEMBERS of this FAMILY and their VISITORS, BOARDERS, SERVANTS, &c., who slept or abode in this House on the night of SUNDAY, the 2nd of APRIL, 1911.

24 Duncairn Gardens, Duncairn, Co Antrim

1911 Census in Northern Ireland for Maguire Family. Was his mother born in County Durham or County Dublin?

(Author's collection)

Christian Name	Surname	RELATION to Head of Family	RELIGIOUS PROFESSION	EDUCATION	Age of Males	Age of Females	RANK, PROFESSION, OR OCCUPATION	Whether "Married," "Widower," "Widow," or "Single"	Completed years the present Marriage has lasted	Total Children born alive	Children still living	WHERE BORN	IRISH LANGUAGE
Henry	Maguire	Head of Family	Roman Catholic	Read and Write	60		Plasterer	Married				Co Down	
Mary L.J.	Maguire	Wife	Roman Catholic	Read and Write		55		Married	30	One	One	Co Durh.	
Henry	Maguire	Son	Roman Catholic	Read and Write	27		Civil Engineer	Single				Belfast	

I hereby certify, as required by the Act 10 Edw. VII., and 1 Geo. V., cap. 11, that the foregoing Return is correct, according to the best of my knowledge and belief.

Anthony William   Signature of Enumerator.

I believe the foregoing to be a true Return.

Henry Maguire   Signature of Head of Family.

Medal Role Card for Henry
Maguire
(Crown Copyright -
Author's collection)

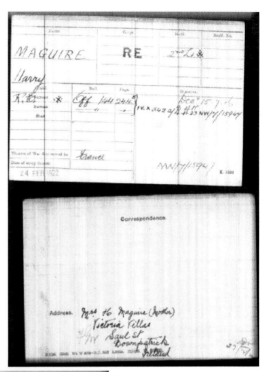

Memorial to the
38th Welsh Division
at Mametz Wood
with whom Henry
fought and died.
(Author's collection)

Private Alec Richardson
(Courtesy of Wolsingham School)

Richardson gravestone in Witton
le Wear Cemetery.
(Author's collection)

Wear Terrace, Witton le Wear showing Langstaff timber yard at the end of the terrace houses.
(Author's collection)

Wear Terrace where so many of Witton le Wear's young soldiers lived.
(Author's collection)

Marriage certificate of Bertram Randall and Edith Pegg in Witton le Wear
Parish Church. 25th December 1915.
(Author's collection)

Postcard of the 'Fighting Fifth' otherwise known as the Northumberland Fusiliers after the Battle of St Eloi in 1916, south of Ypres. The steel helmets had
only been recently issued.
(Author's collection)

Gravestone of Bertram Randall,
Mont Huon Cemetery, France
(Courtesy of the
Rowland Family)

In Memory of

Corporal

Bertram Arthur Randall

1492, 1st Bn., Northumberland Fusiliers
who died on 01 December 1917 Age 30
Husband of Edith Frances Randall, of 11, West End, Witton-le-Wear, Co. Durham.

Remembered with Honour
Mont Huon Military Cemetery, Le Treport

Commemorated in perpetuity by
the Commonwealth War Graves Commission

Copy of an online memorial
certificate provided by the
CWGC for Bertram Randall
(Author's collection)

1917: Timeline on the Western Front

15 March
Czar Nicholas II of Russia abdicates

6 April
America declares war on Germany

9 April
Canadian success at Battle of Vimy Ridge

16 July – 10 November
Third Battle of Ypres also known as Passchendaele Offensive

7 November
Russian Revolution and Lenin comes to power

20 November
Battle of Cambrai – first successful tank battle for the British

1 December
Corporal Bertram Randall dies at Le Treport

Bertram Randall

'This little wayside station o'ergrown with fragrant flowers,
The red-roofed white washed cottages, thy cool and shady bowers;
The cattle grazing quietly within the pastures near,
Make thee a pretty picture, bonnie Witton le Wear.'

Bertram Arthur Randall was born in Cardiff, Glamorgan, in December 1887 and moved to Birmingham prior to 1891. At the age of 13, he was living in digs in Handsworth, Staffordshire with his engine fitter father and his older brother Thomas (often called Alfred) who was also an engine fitter. Bertram was working as an errand boy.

When old enough, Bertram enlisted in the regular army at Canterbury and his designated army number, 1492 stayed with him till the end of his life. By 1911, he was with the 3rd Northumberland Fusiliers (Special Reserve Battalion) in the barracks at Barrack Road, Newcastle and on the census was recorded as a single man, aged 23. Unfortunately his army records were destroyed in the London blitz in 1940, but Bertram was promoted to Corporal.

Bertram's story comes from census, marriage certificates, medal rolls, battalion war diaries and Commonwealth War Graves Commission information. As he was not awarded the 1914/15 Star, he was not on active service abroad and during the early part of the war he was on home service. Bertram's marriage certificate shows he was living in East Boldon, with the 3rd Battalion of the Northumberland Fusiliers when he married Edith Francis Pegg on the 25th December 1915 in the parish church in Witton le Wear. This was not a marriage under special license but under normal circumstances with the timely calling of the banns. Bertram was a 28 year old bachelor and a soldier and his bride Edith, was a 28 year old spinster with no recorded employment. She must have been resident in the parish at the time of the wedding. Witnesses were William Pegg (probably her father) and Isabel Winnifred Randall.

Edith had been born and brought up in Carlton Scroop, Lincolnshire and her father was a railway signaller and linesman. In 1911, her widowed father was still living in Carlton Scroop with Edith's older sister Mary. Edith was working as sewing maid with the wealthy Wells-Cole family in Skellingthorpe, Lincolnshire. How she came to Witton le Wear is a puzzle. Maybe she met Bertram when he was on army service in Lincolnshire, maybe both fathers knew each other with their link to trains, or maybe she changed employers and moved to the village.

Bertram and Edith set up home at 11 West End, Witton le Wear and could not have spent very long together as husband and wife. We do not know when, but he was sent overseas with the 1st Battalion of the Northumberland Fusiliers fairly soon after their marriage.

The Northumberland Fusiliers, known as the 'Fighting Fifth' raised 51 battalions during the Great War and was one of the largest regiments in the British Army. The 1st and 2nd Battalions were regular army soldiers, the 3rd Battalion was the training unit stationed in East Boldon and Sunderland, and the other battalions were made up of territorial soldiers and conscripts. Bertram was transferred to the 1st Battalion and was sent to France where he took part in some very heavy fighting during 1916 and 1917 at the northern end of the western front. These included the Battles of Albert, Bazentin, Delville Wood, and Ancre which were part of the Somme offensive, and in 1917, Battle of Arras, the Third Battle of Ypres and the Battle of Cambrai. The total strength of the Battalion in

October 1917 was 40 officers, 5 warrant officers, 6 staff sergeants, 50 sergeants, 10 lance sergeants, 70 corporals, 90 lance corporals and 682 privates which totalled 914 men. One of these Corporals was Bertram Randall.

The war diary of November 1917, was not written in army issue diary pages, instead it only covered several days from 20th November onwards and was written in jotter form, possibly from an officer's own notepad. The diary indicates several days of very heavy fighting between the 20th and 22nd November, when the Northumberland Fusiliers attacked enemy trenches and the enemy counter attacked their trenches, making for harrowing reading. This fighting took place in the Norevil area of the Cambrai Salient. 18 men were killed including three officers, 84 were wounded, 30 were wounded severely enough to be sent to casualty clearing stations and 9 were classed as missing. Bertram was one of the 30 injured men sent to the casualty clearing station for treatment on the 21st or 22nd November. After treatment at the clearing station, Bertram was transferred by field ambulance to Le Treport on the North Sea coast which was an important hospital centre. There were 3 hospitals here and it was here that Bertram died on the 1st December 1917. As the Le Treport cemetery had been filled, he was buried in the Mont Huon Military Cemetery. There are 2128 WWI graves in this cemetery and there are also 200 German war graves.

How Edith was informed of the death of her husband is not known, but most likely she received the dreaded knock on the door at her home in 11 West End, and the telegram. It was unlikely that she would have had her family around to support her, but her married life to Bertram had been short and they became part of 'the lost generation'. It is not known if Edith married again at a later date.

The Rowland family who lived in 11 West End in 2005, read about Bertram in the village newsletter, "Witton Word" and they did not know about the man who previously lived in their home. They visited France during the summer and made a special visit to Bertram's grave and took a photograph.

At the bottom of the stone is written

> *"Thy purpose Lord*
> *we cannot see*
> *But all is well*
> *That's done by thee"*

Families were allowed to add text to the gravestones if they wished at the cost of 3½ pence per letter. This means that Edith will have paid for 53 letters – 15 shillings and 5½ pence for the inscription on the stone.

Bertram was the only soldier from the village to die in 1917 and his name is on the Witton le Wear War Memorial.

1918 – 1919: Timeline on the Western Front

3 March
Russia and Central Powers sign peace treaty

21 March - May
German advance on Western Front

21 March
John Saunders reported missing, presumed killed near Bapaume

23 March
Frederick Hall reported missing at Lebucquiere and his body presumed to be one of the unidentified buried in the cemetery.

30 April
Christopher Whitton dies at Le Treport

31 May
James Coates dies at Abeele

June – September
Allies start pushing German army back towards Germany through Hindenburg Line
 Battle of Amiens (August)

19 September – 3 November
Bulgaria sign armistice with allies
Turks sign armistice with allies
Austria – Hungary sign armistice with allies

25 September
George Walton Scott is killed at Messines

10 October
Albert Dean MC is killed at Comines

3 November
Harry Langstaff dies of wounds at Rouen

9 November
Kaiser Wilhelm II of Germany abdicates

11 November
Fighting ends with the signing of the armistice between Allies and Germany

1919

1 February
Thomas Stobbs dies at Edingen, Belgium

John Thomas Sanders

'Let others boast of landscapes which no doubt are very nice,
But thou are far superior, superb earthly paradise;
The perfume of the meadow-lanes, thy bracing atmosphere,
Will live with me my whole life long, fair Witton le Wear.'

John is remembered on the gravestone where his mother is buried in Witton le Wear Cemetery.

'Sanders Jane, wife of William Snaith Sanders,
died 5th February 1938 aged 78 years,
also of John Thomas, her son reported missing in the Great War,
21st March 1918, aged 27 years.'

John was born in 1890 in Etherley and the family moved to Witton Park. He had one younger brother Daniel. John's father had spent much of his childhood in Witton le Wear with an uncle, Edward Snaith, his Aunt Mary and cousins John and William hence the Witton connection[12]. In 1901[13], the family was living in Phoenix Row, near Witton Park and by 1911[14] they were at 6 Black Road, Witton Park and John's profession was a draper's assistant.

His army records are available, faint in places but fairly well detailed. John volunteered for enlistment on 11th December 1915, took his oath of allegiance in Sunderland and served with the 2nd Durham Light Infantry. He was 5 foot 5 inches tall and 25 years and 3 months old when he enlisted. It appears he was unfit for service overseas at this time so served on the Army Reserve from 12th December 1915 until 23rd August 1917. This was common as the general health of many young men was poor and many suffered rickets, flat feet and had poor nutrition. In January 1917, John was admitted to

---

[12] 1871 census
[13] 1901 census
[14] 1911 census

hospital with scabies where he stayed for 2 days. On the 24th August 1917, he began active training for frontline service and on the 27 January 1918, John was shipped to France where in less than 2 months he would be classed as missing whilst fighting with the 'Durhams' in the 6th Division.

The war diary for the 2nd Battalion Durham Light Infantry reveals the horrors of what happened. As well as the diary, there are hand written reports by the colonel, and typed reports by two of the Lieutenants describing the events of the 21st – 23rd March, one written in India in 1922 and it was obviously still very vivid in his memory. Of the 30 officers and 639 other ranks that were present on the morning of 21st March 1918, 28 officers and 571 men were killed, wounded or captured by the end of the day. It was reported that of the 1600 men of all ranks who went into action on the morning of the 21st, 80 men came out on the morning of the 23rd. John was one of soldiers who were classed as missing and his body was never found.

John is remembered with honour on the Arras Memorial which commemorates 35,000 servicemen with no known grave from the United Kingdom, South Africa and New Zealand who died in the Arras sector between the spring 1916 and August 1918. The Commonwealth War Graves Commission has recorded John as being Joseph T Sanders, but there is no doubt that this is our John from Witton Park. He is also remembered on the Witton Park War Memorial situated in the village cemetery.

The 21st March 1918 was the first day of the final German offensive to try to retake France and Flanders. It was particularly ferocious and many soldiers on both sides died over the next 3 months before the allies forced the Germans to retreat. The 2nd Durham Light Infantry had a major presence at this time in the Beugnatre area, 3 kilometres from Bapaume and Lieutenant McBain was an eye witness to the following events on the 21st March 1918.

"On the 19th and 20th March it was abnormally quiet regarding enemy gun and rifle fire, but the allies could hear the enemy bringing up ammunition and stores ready for an attack. The wire fencing in front of the allied trenches was reinforced by the pioneer battalion of old soldiers. Lieutenant McBain was battalion bombing officer and found himself in battalion HQ on the morning of the 21st. An 18 pounder gun was placed in the reserve line to meet any enemy tanks and the ground in front of the front line had been strewn with medium trench mortar bombs intended to explode if tanks passed over them.

At 4am, a heavy enemy barrage commenced on both the front and the battle line. Half of the shells contained gas, so respirators had to be worn from the commencement of the battle, even although a high number of enemy shells failed to explode. Buried cables leading to brigade headquarters and forward lines that were 6 feet deep were severed by shell fire at 7am and therefore communication lines were cut. Runners were used to try to keep communication lines open and pigeons were used to keep Brigade Headquarters informed of the dire situation. One runner reported at 7.30am from the left front company that the enemy was attacking and heavy casualties had been sustained by the forward companies. This was the only man who ever came back from the front line to Lieutenant McBain's knowledge, and he returned to his comrades as soon as the message was delivered.

It was impossible to see what the situation was in the front line at this time owing to the heavy mist and the bombardment. By 9.30am the mist had lifted sufficiently to show that the front lines had been captured. Large numbers of the enemy could be seen in close order moving towards the right flank. Artillery and wagons could also be seen moving forward amidst the bursting shells of allied heavy gunfire.

Shortly after 10am, German bombs were thrown along the entrance to the allied battalion headquarters and the staff, signallers and runners made for the back entrance where they made exit into another trench. Here a counter attack was organized and Lieutenant McBain, Lance Corporal Berry and Private Keech found two boxes of bombs and used them to clear the Germans from the trenches. They set up a block and sent back for reinforcements and Headquarters was back in allied hands.

German troops continued to advance and they reached the high ground and set up a machine gun which could sweep along the allied reserve lines. At 6pm Lieutenant McBain received orders to withdraw with his men as the enemy was surrounding them on three sides."

In his written account, Lieutenant McBain pointed out that the 2nd Durham Light Infantry was the only battalion in the front line of the division and probably in the Fourth Corp that held its battle positions for the whole of the 21st March and only retired when ordered to do so.

Lieutenant Hutchinson wrote a description of the battle of the 21st March 1918 when he was in Sialkot, India in 1927 and he had obviously read other reports of the day the Germans started the final offensive – the last 100 days.

"On the 21st March, just before 4am, the battle began with a tremendous crash on a front of 70 kilometres. The eastern sky blazed from end to end and then the whole front appeared to be deluged in bursting shells.

Till 9am, our trenches were deluged in a hurricane of bursting shells. chiefly whizz-bangs and 5.9's. The front line suffered very heavy casualties, but the barrage on the reserve trench was not well aimed and the casualties were not excessive, considering the weight of the bombardment. At 9am the hostile batteries concentrated to form a barrage and their infantry advanced to the assault. By 10am the front line and close supports, battered to pieces by the bombardment, its garrison destroyed or captured, was in the enemy's hands, not a man escaping to give warning to the companies in reserve. By 10.30am, the Germans were pouring into the valley between the lines and reached Battalion Headquarters. Bombs bursting in and around this dug-out was the first intimation of the attack and for a time it looked as if Headquarters was doomed. Attempts were made to recapture it, and eventually 2nd Lieutenant McBain assisted by Private Keech made a counter attack with bombs, killing about 30 of the enemy, taking four machine guns. This completely cowed the nearest attackers and saved the battalion front until evening.

By late afternoon, the situation was as follows: On the battalion front all opposition had been broken in advance of the reserve line trench. On the right the West Yorks were outflanked and holding their own with difficulty, while on the left the Germans penetrated the defences almost to Vaulx

Vrancourt, a very considerable distance to the rear. This being the situation and the last of the reserves of the brigade, and the 11th Essex having been thrown into fill up the two miles gap between the West Yorks and the 51st Division, a duty they were too weak to perform. Lieutenant Colonel Brereton seeing that of the two companies left to him, nearly all experienced officers and NCOs were either killed or wounded, decided to retire at dusk.

All arrangements were made for the withdrawal, when the enemy bringing up reinforcements, drove the West Yorks into the battalion sector in confusion. This precipitated the withdrawal, which had to be carried out in daylight under heavy machine gun fire. Although barely 50 men survived the ordeal, the withdrawal was carried out in good order.

Lieutenant Colonel Brereton, Commanding Officer of the 2nd DLI wrote in his report regarding the two front companies (where John had been fighting) whose orders were to hold until the last man. The only two who left the line were two officers who were wounded early in the morning and who after having their wounds dressed, reported to Battalion Headquarters for duty along with one man who accompanied them to the first aid post. Everyone else died or was posted as missing. None of the men of the wiring platoon or the signallers returned. The gallantry of all the officers and men who died was mentioned in the report.

On 28th March, King George V visited the 6th division and the following is recorded.

"His Majesty THE KING, this afternoon paid a visit to the 6th Division and talked to the officers and the men who had taken part in the recent fighting. On departure, THE KING asked the Divisional Commander to let the Division know how much he appreciated their magnificent defence on the 21st and 22nd. He wished them all luck, and was sure that he could depend on them to fight as well again.

The Divisional Commander is sure that all ranks will; proudly remember the honour done to them by this special visit of His Majesty, and is confident that they will uphold in future actions the splendid reputation for fighting which they have won throughout the war and added to in the recent battles of CAMBRAI and BAPAUME.

Lt Colonel P Hudson, AA &QMG, 6th Division"

So we have a local lad, who was not very robust, who volunteered for the army as all his friends would have done. He stayed at home working in the local drapers shop, and only in 1918 when the army was desperate for soldiers was he sent to war. What did he experience in the two months active front line service can only be imagined and for this - his mother was sent his death plaque, and a Victory and British War Medal? As his body was never found, it must have been some comfort to her to have John's name engraved on the Witton Park War Memorial to which she could walk from her home. She also had left instructions for his name to be included on her gravestone in Witton le Wear Cemetery, so in her small way, she ensured that his memory would live on.

Frederick Hall

'The scenery I will ne'er forget; it thrills my heart and brain,
How can so many visit thee and yet no profit gain;
The sweetest joy that I could tell, or music I could hear,
Could not please me more than thee, fair Witton le Wear.'

Frederick Hall is remembered on the Witton le Wear War Memorial and researching him provided a different challenge. It was easy to determine that he was born in Bishop Auckland in July 1895. In 1901, Fred was living with his grandparents William and Eleanor Burn in Victoria House, Witton le Wear. William was a Jersey cattle importer and farmer who employed his 30 year old niece, Mary Thompson as a dairymaid, and had a stockman and domestic servant also living in the house.

Fred's mother was Mary Burn, daughter of William and Eleanor and she married Frederic Alfred Hall in the summer of 1894 in Bishop Auckland. He was storekeeper and another son Reginald Robert Hall was born in Bishop Auckland in April 1899. After this the family moved to 132 Joan Street, Benwell, Newcastle and a third son Faraday Franklin Hall was born in 1904.

Fred however was still living in Witton le Wear in 1911 with his, by now widowed grandmother. After leaving school he went on to work as a clerk for the engineers department of the North Eastern Railway at Bishop Auckland.

Frederic, Fred's father died early in 1912 at the age of 44 and Mary moved to 5 Albert Hill, Bishop Auckland. On the 26th April 1917, Fred's brother Reginald, reached the age of 18 and immediately enlisted in the 2nd West Riding Regiment and was sent to the Western Front. In December, he was promoted in the field to Lance Corporal. His records are available but are extremely poor and most of them are illegible. Reginald was medically discharged in December 1918 and awarded a disability pension. He came home to his mother in Bishop Auckland but it looks as though he died prior to 18th March 1919, as when his mother received Reginald's war medal through the post, she signed the receipt form as mother of the deceased soldier.

Fred had enlisted in the Army Reserve on the 6th December 1915 at Helmsley and was 5 foot 8 inches tall, had a 35 inch chest with 2 inch expansion, and had no distinctive features. He was posted to the 1st Battalion Kings Royal Rifle Corps and although his army records survive, they are of a very poor quality and difficult to interpret. Fred was with the 21st Service Battalion and sent to join the British Expeditionary Force in France on 5th May 1916. In November 1917 he served in Italy and in early March 1918, he returned to France and fought with the 1st Battalion Kings Royal Rifles in the Somme region.

The final German offensive started on the 21st March and the fighting was unrelenting with massive casualties on both sides. Fred was reported missing on the 23rd March 1918. Later in the day, the records state he was accepted as having died, having served 2 years and 11 days in army service. Many soldiers were listed as missing although some did reappear alive and battle weary, but this was not the case for Fred. Soldiers were blown up by shell or mortar fire or their bodies sunk deep into the mud of no-man's land. Stretcher bearers from the battalions and the Royal Army Medical Corps did their very best but often during battles it was impossible to bring back wounded and dead soldiers. Almost 100 years after this bloody conflict, bodies are still reappearing in the fields in Flanders. The remains are treated with the greatest respect and every attempt is made to try to identify the soldier to allow the family to pay their respects when the remains are laid to rest in a nearby cemetery.

When possible, dead soldiers were buried as soon as possible and in many cases they had no identification on them as their single dog tag could have been removed or disappeared in the chaos of war. It was about this time that soldiers were issued with two dog tags to ensure that one stayed with the body to help with identification. Fred was buried as an unknown soldier, but following the war, bodies were brought into the larger cemetery at Lebucquiere and Fred is believed to be buried in one of the special memorial graves in the cemetery extension.

Fred's address on his army records was 5 Albert Hill Terrace in Bishop Auckland, and when the army wrote to his mother about this medals and scroll, the address was over written with: Mrs M.M. Hall, c/o Mrs Burns, Victoria House, Witton le Wear. The relationship between Mary and her son Fred is unclear and the records indicate that he spent his childhood in Witton le Wear with grandparents rather than with his parents in Newcastle.

The war memorial in Bishop Auckland is a generic marble memorial which is currently situated in the market place in Bishop Auckland and there is a memorial book kept within St Anne's Church donated by the Eden Theatre Heroes Memorial Fund as a permanent memorial. This book has the names of all of fallen from Bishop Auckland including Fred Hall.

Fred is also remembered on the North Eastern Railway Memorial at York as an employee of N.E.R.

He is also remembered on the war memorial within St Peter's Church in Princes Street, Bishop Auckland as one of the 86 men of the parish who gave their lives during WWI. His brother, Reginald is named on this memorial too although he does not seem to be recorded on any of the other war memorials which contain Fred's name including the one in Witton le Wear Parish Church. The reason for this is unclear. It is fair to presume that as Fred spent his childhood years with his grandparents in Victoria House, Witton le Wear, his grandmother would want his name on the village memorial. He was known as a 'Witton boy'. Reginald theoretically was not classed as 'war dead' as he had been discharged from the army, so was not seen as being one of the 'fallen' soldiers, although there can be little doubt that his wartime injuries would have been a significant factor in his death at the age of 19 years. There appears to have been a family rift as Reginald is not mentioned in Fred's army records as a brother although Faraday's name is present. Maybe the brothers had little in common and barely knew each other.

Whatever the reasons for the split, Mary Hall lost two of her three sons. One son was missing presumed dead and the other came back from war, old before his years and died within a few months. How glad she must have been that Faraday was too young to go to war. How sad Eleanor Burns must have been for the lost years of her grandsons?

Christopher Whitton

'There is knowledge in the thistle, and wisdom in the thorn,
Just as sure as there is hope in the growing, waving corn;
There is life in every flower, to fill other lives with cheer,
They adorn thy riverbanks, dear Witton le Wear.'

Christopher Whitton was born in Witton le Wear at the end of 1886 and was known within the family as Kit.   He was remembered in Witton le Wear Cemetery on the grave of his father, also called Christopher, who died in 1926 and his stepmother, Margaret Jane who died in 1942.

and their son
CHRISTOPHER JAMES WHITTON,
6th Battalion DLI
who died of wounds in France,
April 30th 1918, aged 31 years.

Kit's name also appears on the War Memorial in St Catherine's Parish Church in Crook.

Kit's mother died when he was a baby and his father married Margaret Jane from Lanchester in 1889 and went on to have five more children, George Matthew born 1894, Mark born 1897, Mary born January 1901, Florence Ada born January 1903 and John born April 1909.   They were all born in Witton le Wear except Mark who was born in Crook. In 1901[15], the family lived at Victoria Cottages, Howden le Wear and both Kit and his father were coal miners.   The family were still living here in 1911[16] but had been joined by Kit's 77 year old grandfather who was a widower and young George was by this time also working in the coal mines.   By 1918, the family was living at Red House, Roddymoor.

---

[15] 1901 census
[16] 1911 census

There is very little known about Kit's army career as his army records are lost, the war diaries of 6th battalion DLI are sparse and the main information has been obtained from the Commonwealth War Graves Commission and North East Memorials Project. This project was set up in 2000 and there is an extensive searchable database of almost all the war memorials in the North East which provides a very useful source of information.

Kit enlisted and was posted to the 6th Battalion, Durham Light Infantry which served in Flanders and France. He was most likely a Territorial soldier with the Durham Light Infantry prior to the war, as his original army number was four digits 3787. In 1911, Kit was working as a miner at the age of 24, and many miners were also in the Territorial Army and joined up for active service at the beginning of the war. It is not known when Kit went to France but as he died in April 1918, the war diary for this month, and Ward's 'Faithful – The Story of the Durham Light Infantry' gives additional details to what occurred at this time to the 6th DLI as part of the 151st Brigade and 50th Division. In April 1918, the Germans had begun their final push to capture Flanders and France.

During the nights of the 1st – 7th April, the DLI soldiers marched from Gentelles, near Amien, to Beuvry, south of Bethune, and then travelled the last 12 miles by train to Estaires, west of Armentieres a total of 100 miles. The majority of movement took place during the night as it was less susceptible to enemy fire power. On the morning of the 8th April, they were billeted in Estaires and at 4.30am were ordered to 'stand to' in anticipation of an enemy attack. This attack did not materialize and the rest of the day was quiet. At 4am, the following morning, Estaires was heavily bombed and the 1/6th

Durhams lost all but five of its officers when a shell struck the convent in which they were billeted. That morning Kit and his comrades went into action with Major Heslop, four officers, and all its platoons and one company commanded by non-commissioned officers. They fought valiantly and initially held fortified farms and posts 2 miles south east of Estaires, but the 6th received heavy casualties and were reduced to four officers and 60 men and as a result fell back to the River Lys. On the 10th April, the Germans took Estaires, and by the 11th, the enemy outnumbered the allies four to one.

It was reported that the Germans found large quantities of alcohol in Estaires and they partied all night. The rowdy singing could be heard by the allies entrenched nearby. These excesses caused delay in the attack planned for the 11th, but on the 12th April, the Germans attacked in even greater strength. The DLI fought so stubbornly that by 3pm when thirteen fresh allied battalions arrived, the Germans had only gained 1500 yards. During the early hours of the 13th, the DLI were relieved and moved back into the reserve line. The fighting had been over a 10 mile area and the war diary does not indicate how many men were killed or wounded, but on the 17th April, they were visited by the Divisional General Officer in command who thanked them for their work in recent operations. He was reported to have said that the fine stand of the 50th division during the 4 days of battle had gained the necessary time to enable the reserves to be brought forward. The cost of this was unfortunately, the almost annihilation of the battalion.   On the 20th a new draft of 200 men and 9 officers arrived in the 6thDLI and immediately began training and refitting ready for the next onslaught.

It is highly likely that during these four days of unrelenting fighting, Kit was wounded. After treatment in the Casualty Clearing Station, Kit was moved to hospital at Le Treport on the North Sea coast. His condition deteriorated and he died of his wounds on the 30th April 1918 and was buried at Mont Huon Military Cemetery.

James Coates

'While toiling in silence in the darkness of the mine,
Locked in the bowels of the earth for thee I oft repine;
My thoughts which can ne'er be entombed will often bring me here,
To live again this happy day near Witton le Wear.'

James Coates is not listed on the village war memorial in Witton le Wear, but he was born in the village so has been included within this book.

He was born in Witton le Wear in 1884, the youngest child of William and Mary Coates, a family which originated from Swaledale in Yorkshire. He had two older brothers, Thomas and Lenorat and a sister, Jane Ann. By the time James was seven years old, he was living at 54 High Grange where William and Thomas were coal miners and Lenorat, Jane Ann and James were at school. The family cannot be found on the 1901 census which could be an error in digitisation or they may have been out of the country as they do not appear on the English, Welsh or Scottish census.

In July 1906, James married Hannah from Willington, County Durham. They had 2 daughters, Mary born in 1907 and Doris born in 1908, and by 1911 they were living at Constantine Road, North Bitchburn. James like his father was a hewer in the coal mines.

James enlisted in the East Yorkshire Regiment and on the 27th August 1915 was sent to France. Being a miner, he was at some time transferred to the Royal Engineers where his mining skills were soon being used within the 255th Tunnelling Regiment. These men were sent down to dig tunnels below German lines with the ultimate aim of blowing them and their occupants up. This was extremely stressful and dangerous. In

Geoff Dyer's book 'The Missing of the Somme', he described miners finding themselves engaged in exactly the same activity they had pursued in peacetime, except that here their aim in burrowing below the earth was to lay hundreds of pounds of high explosives beneath the enemy's feet. The Germans meanwhile were engaged in similar operations and sometimes the two tunnel systems broke into each other. Hundreds of feet beneath the surface, men clawed at each other's throats and beat each other to death with picks and shovels. The miners used to say as long as you could hear the enemy scraping you could rest easy, but when it went quiet, it was the time to get worried as the miners would leave the mine before setting off the explosives.

It was not underground that James died, but during the early hours of 31st May, the area in which he was repairing trenches and wiring, Boeschepe Lane, east of Abeele, suffered severe shelling and 35 soldiers were killed or injured. The war diary states that on the 31st May, half of the section was deployed in digging graves for their dead comrades. James had been injured and was taken to the casualty clearing station at Lijssenthoek, near Poperinge where he died and was buried in Lijssenthoek Military Cemetery.

Back at the family home at 8 Low Row, North Bitchburn, Hannah received notification of James's death. Mary at this time was aged 11 and Doris aged 9. Life would have been hard for the family with just an army pension but in 1922, Hannah Coates married Thomas Slack in the Auckland area so it can be hoped that Hannah did find happiness again.

James is remembered on the Howden le Wear Parish Church memorial that was saved by the local history group when the church was sold in 2009. His name is also on the Howden le Wear war memorial in the centre of the village. Interestingly the memorial states his regiment was the East Yorkshire Regiment and not the Royal Engineers. Village war memorials were provided by public subscription and the information to be inscribed would be supplied by the families, which sometimes meant there were anomalies when regiments do not always appear the same as the army records. It may show the Coates family allegiance to Yorkshire.

Hannah was sent James's medals - 1914/15 Star, Victory Medal, the British Medal and his death plaque.

George Walton Scott

'Many who have left thee for some distant shore,
Still look back with longing to the far off days of yore;
And when their thoughts are turned to thee, with many a heartfelt tear,
They wish that they were back again at Witton on the Wear.'

George Walton Scott was born on 11th September 1897 in Forest and Frith parish, Teesdale, second son of Thomas and Mary Jane Scott, a family of lead miners. A visit to Killhope Lead Mines in Upper Weardale shows how these lead miners and their families lived in the 19th century, just as it would have been for the Scott family. Thomas was away Monday to Friday in the mines living in the shared lodging house with umpteen other men and boys, and only coming home at weekends to Mary Jane who managed the small rented farm. Life was hard but to all accounts these were happy days. Mary Jane was a devout Methodist and she spent time cleaning the Wesleyan Chapel. As their family grew up, they were all expected to do their share and attend chapel every Sunday and take an active part in the Sunday school. Lead mining declined at the end of the 19th century and by 1914 the Scott family were living at Institute House in Witton le Wear.

George was not immune to the call for volunteers and he enlisted at Bishop Auckland with the Lancashire Fusiliers and later moved to the 2nd Battalion of the South Lancashire Regiment (Prince of Wales Volunteers). George came home on leave from the Western Front in July 1918 following being gassed and wounded twice[17]. He sent a telegram from Kings Cross station to his parents stating 'I am coming home tonight late.' It was sent at 4.20pm on the 29th July and was franked 6.45pm in Witton le Wear. There must have been great

---

[17] Auckland Chronicle, 15th August 1918

excitement and many of his family members would possibly be down at Witton le Wear station when his train arrived in the village.

We do not know much about George's army career but there is a record in the regimental war diaries, of the events involving the Battalion at the time he died. In September 1918, the 2nd Battalion of the South Lancashire Regiment was fighting in the Messines region of Flanders, about 8 miles south of Ypres. The war diary for this time is extremely detailed and outlines several episodes of heroism including one where the Military Cross was later awarded to a Lieutenant Harrison who was killed the following day. When Tuesday 24th dawned, the weather was reported as being 'fine'. Heavy rain had been experienced during the night and life in the trenches was very difficult when the rain had turned the trenches into muddy quagmires. It is known that George was killed on Wednesday 25th September 1918. The war diary identifies that four men from George's battalion died on the 25th September, all being other ranks, i.e. not officers. George was buried in Wulverghem Lindenhoek Road Military Cemetery. His grave was inscribed with the badge of the South Lancashire Regiment and the following words:

34510 Private G. W. Scott
South Lancashire Regiment
25th September 1918, aged 21

Below this is a cross and at the bottom of the stone, the family had inscribed:

'He rests in peace'

The grave next to George holds the body of Corporal George Cockshoot from Darwen, Shrewsbury, who died the same day as George Scott and they had fought shoulder to shoulder in 'D' company. George Cockshoot had received the Military Medal for bravery in battle on June 1918 which was awarded posthumously to his parents on the 8th June 1919. Both soldiers saw a high level of enemy action, were battle hardened, and when they died they were buried in a small local cemetery nearby. At the end of the war, their bodies were exhumed together and moved to Wulverghem-Lindenhoek Cemetery by the Imperial War Graves Commission. One other soldier who died during the same battle as George was buried in the same cemetery, Private B Bentley and the fourth soldier, Private Francis Pell was buried at Westoutre British Cemetery.

Back in Witton le Wear his parents received the much dreaded telegram fairly quickly after George died. A letter was received by his mother from 2nd Lieutenant H.V. Kitching[18] It said:

> *"It is with much regret I have to inform you of the loss of your son in action on the 25th September. He was doing very good work at the time and I should like to add I have always found him a boy with plenty of pluck and excellent spirit. You have my deepest sympathy. You may like to know that were able to give him a burial behind the line quickly shortly afterwards."*

In the absence of a family funeral, a memorial service was held in the Wesleyan Methodist Chapel in Witton le Wear on Sunday 3rd November. George's belongings were returned within several months and the family eventually received his medals, an inscribed death plaque and certificate.

---

[18] Auckland Chronicle, 10th October 1918

A letter was also received by the family conveying the King's sympathy which was cherished by his mother for the rest of her life. Witton le Wear also had a 'Welcome Home Fund' which gave a small gift to returning soldiers. Mrs Scott was given the choice to buy something in memory of George and she chose a clock which nearly 100 years later is still in the possession of the family.

Albert Dean MC

'Lovely place, I now must go, night is drawing nigh,
The orb of day now goes to rest, thy glory fills the sky;
But when the clouds have lost their tints and twinkling stars appear,
I shall have pleasant dreams of thee, fair Witton le Wear.'

Albert's story is of a different form of heroism. His link to Witton le Wear is that he is remembered on his father's grave in the village cemetery.

'In loving memory of Joseph, the beloved husband of Elizabeth Dean
of Bishop Auckland, who died October 13th 1915 aged 63 years. Also of
their son Albert Dean MC, killed in France, October 10th 1918 aged 34 years.'

Albert is also remembered on the war memorial in St Anne's Church in Bishop Auckland.

Albert Dean was born on 5th November 1883 at the family home - 13 Newgate Street, Bishop Auckland to Joseph and Elizabeth Dean. Joseph was a grocer in partnership with a Mr Johnson and the grocers shop was also at 13 Newgate Street[19]. Elizabeth and Joseph had 4 children but the two girls Annie Lilian, aged 13 and Ethel aged 8 years both died in childhood leaving Albert and his older brother William. In 1901[20] the family moved to Clarence Villas where William was classed as a grocer's assistant and working with his father. William later married and had one son and continued as a grocer in the family business Dean and Son situated in Bishop Auckland after his father's death. By the 1911 census the family and business moved to 53 Market Place, Bishop Auckland[21] and Albert was still living at home.

---

[19] 1881 census and 1891 census
[20] 1901 census
[21] 1911 census

Albert became a lithographic artist working in the local printing industry and by 1914[22] he had set up his own label printing business 'Allan and Dean' with John Allen situated in Cocktonhill Road, in Bishop Auckland.

Albert was enticed by the patriotic spirit that swept through the town and enlisted, taking his attestation oath on 22nd February 1915 in Darlington. He was assigned as a driver in the Royal Engineers. At this time he was 30 years and 3 months old, his height was 5 foot 3¼ inches, his chest expansion was 2½ inches and his weight was 115 lbs. On 4th March, he commenced 7 months home service and was transferred to the 126th Field Company of the Royal Engineers. At the end of the month Albert was promoted to lance corporal and he must have continued to show leadership qualities as on 26th August, Albert was promoted to full Corporal. On 11th September 1915, he went with the British Expeditionary Force to the Western Front having seen his father for the last time, as Joseph died one month later.

Albert must have been a good soldier as on the 23rd September 1917 he was transferred back to England to be trained for a temporary commission. He served at Oxford as an officer cadet and graduated on the 2nd May 1918. His report said 'although he was excellent in theory, he was poor in application, but he had worked very hard'. His standard of education was good, and his military knowledge was good. His power of command and leadership was only fair. Albert embarked on 3 July 1918 with the 29th (service) battalion of the Durham Light Infantry for France. The 29th battalion was the last DLI battalion to be formed. It had 11 men of low medical

---

[22] Kelly's Directory 1914

category from a variety of northern regiments including 100 men from the 27th DLI and 167 men from the 28th DLI. Over one third were found to be unfit for overseas service but on the 2nd July 1918, they embarked for Flanders with the 14th Division and were actively fighting from early September.

On the 13th September, patrols made contact with the enemy in the Messines area, south of Ypres, and were forced to withdraw under close machine gun fire and a bombing attack. 2nd Lieutenant Dean handled his men very well and reached base with only 6 casualties and brought back all the wounded. For this action he was awarded the Military Cross.

On the 10th October, the 29th DLI made further attacks on the enemy and on the 12th outside the town of Comines, the Germans captured a post previously held by the 29th. There was constant battling and on the 14th October a severe bombardment of the river crossing caused very heavy casualties on both sides. During the early hours of the 15th, a patrol led by 2nd Lieutenant Dean reached an island in the middle of the river, but they sustained several casualties including Albert who was killed during the battle.

Just three weeks before the Armistice was announced, Albert died after experiencing 28 months of heavy fighting in the trenches. On the gravestone in Witton le Wear, his death was recorded as being the 10th October, but records show it was on the 15th that he died of wounds aged 34.

There are numerous pages in Albert's army records, but the most telling are the telegrams to and from his family. The first telegram was from the War Office early in the morning of the 16th telling Mrs Dean that Albert had been injured. She sent a telegram in response about 6pm asking for more information and on the 17th during the morning she received the final telegram informing of his death. Further letters followed including one sent 9th January 1919 telling her that Albert was buried in Le Kreule British Cemetery, north of Hazebrouck. Once the Portland stone memorials were erected, photographs were taken and sent to the family.

In the army records are many letters written between Elizabeth Dean, her solicitors and the War department. £54.14 shillings was eventually paid into Albert's estate from the War office including 10 shillings a month gratuity for 28 months war service overseas. The gross value of his will was £2451.5 shillings all of which went to his mother.

His military cross is not listed within the medals held in the Durham Light Infantry Museum so it must be presumed that they are still within the family or in a private collection.

Kelly's directories give an insight into what happened to the family businesses in Bishop Auckland after the end of the war. In 1921, John Allan was still in business as a label printer and in 1929, 1934 and 1938; the business was recorded as still being Allan and Dean, label printers. It could be that Albert was such an instrumental part of the setting up of the business that John kept his name within the business's title.

Harry Langstaff

'O' rapturous thought, who can describe these lonely woods of thine,
I dare not try, for it will take and abler pen than mine;
A mass of emerald grandeur, do rivals need thee fear,
There are no other woods like thine, sweet Witton le Wear.'

Harry Langstaff was born March 1896 and lived in Witton le Wear all his life. His parents were George and Mary, part of the Langstaff dynasty that could trace their roots back over 500 years in the village. Harry went to the local primary school and then started at Wolsingham Grammar School on 17th January 1911 at the age of 15, presumably because he had showed some academic promise. He is recorded[23] as being House Games Captain and lacked neither inches nor physique and was a quiet and well-liked boy. Harry left Wolsingham Grammar School shortly before his 17th birthday to work with his father in the family sawmills. Harry and his family lived at Laburnum House in Witton le Wear, directly across the road from his cousin Richard Langstaff who enlisted and survived the war.

Harry's army records and the war diaries of the Durham Light Infantry give details of his service. On the 8th December 1915, aged 19 years and 11 months, Harry enlisted for the Army Reserve at Bishop Auckland. He was called for active service on the 23rd May 1918 aged 22 years of age. At his army medical carried out by the Sunderland Medical Board, he was described as being 5ft 6 inches tall, 143 lbs. fair hair, fresh complexion, and had blue eyes. He had two vaccination scars on his left arm, his eyesight was 6/9 in both eyes which was a little below par, but he did not require spectacles. His chest measurement was 38 inches with an expansion of 3 inches. He had a very good physique, which was probably due to the

---

[23] A History of Wolsingham Grammar School, by Anita Atkinson

hard physical labour at the sawmills. Harry's father died of pneumonia on the 9th January 1914, which was Harry's 18th birthday and as the only son, Harry inherited his father's partnership in the business.

Harry joined the 6th Battalion of the Durham Light Infantry, had no hospital admissions and had no certified entries on his regimental conduct sheet. Between 23rd May 1918 and 28th September he was stationed in the UK undertaking training for overseas service. He had home leave, prior to joining the British Expeditionary Force on 28th September 1918 and the 13th Battalion of the Durham Light Infantry. From 23rd October until 29th October, the 13th Battalion engaged the enemy in the area of Le Cateau and there was very heavy machine gun and rifle fire throughout this time.

On 29th October, and according to his service records, Harry was injured with gunshot wounds to his right leg. This happened during the battalion's last episode of fighting and Harry was transferred to the 5th General Hospital at Rouen where his leg was amputated. On the 30th October the sister on the hospital ward wrote to Harry's mother that the operation was successful and his condition was satisfactory. On 7th November the sister wrote again with the news that Harry had collapsed with heart failure and died on Saturday evening 3rd November about 8pm. She wrote "No one ever heard him complain".[24] Harry was buried in St Sever's Cemetery Extension at Rouen. This cemetery contains 8,345 commonwealth WWI graves.

How a young fit man, who had just travelled to the war zone and was injured felt about losing his leg can only be imagined. It was within days of the end of the war. He had

---

[24] Auckland Chronicle, 14th November 1918

served a total of 2 years and 331 days with the army, made up of 166 days in the reserve, 129 days at basic training and 36 days at the Western Front. His belongings were sent back to his mother and listed as:

"Bible, gospel, cigarette case, court mirror, watch strap and protecar, snuff box, razor, prayer book, 3 badges, pencil, 3 buttons, belt, handkerchief, letters, card, purse, 2 telegrams, French book, regimental card, wallet."

These were returned to his mother on the 29th July 1919. At this time his three sisters were all still living at home, Isabella, aged 28 years, Jane aged 25 years and Bessie aged 19 years. Harry was entitled to the British War Medal and the Victory medal which were eventually sent to Laburnum House with his memorial plaque.

As well as having his name engraved on the Witton le Wear Memorial, Harry's name appears on the Wolsingham School Memorial and he has an oak tree dedicated to his memory in the school grounds.

Thomas Stobbs

'If heaven with its glories is more lovelier than thee,
Then I sincerely hope a place will be prepared for me;
But while I dwell upon this earth be thou far or near,
My heart shall hold a place for thee, sweet Witton on the Wear.'

Thomas Stobbs was born in Chatterley, Wolsingham in March 1890, eldest son of George and Elizabeth Stobbs. In 1901, the family was living at South Bedburn and along with Thomas was Sarah Jane aged 9, John Edward aged 8, Joseph aged 5, Humphrey Greenwell aged 3 and Margaret aged 1. Another sister Ann Elizabeth was born in 1902.

By 1911, George Stobbs had died and Elizabeth, Thomas, his two younger brothers and two of his sisters were living in Wear Terrace, Witton le Wear. Thomas and his brother John were the family wage earners working as labourers in the timber yard owned by the Langstaff family. This means that in 1913 and probably until 1915 both Thomas and Harry Langstaff would have been working at the sawmills, one a labourer and the other the owner's son. It was a small business so it is highly possible that they worked side by side. The family later moved to Grey Mare House, 6 West End, Witton le Wear.

There is little information about Thomas as his army records are some of those lost in the WWII blitz; his medal roll card only tells us he was entitled to the Victory Medal and the British medal which tells us he saw active service on the Western Front. Thomas enlisted in Bishop Auckland and was posted to the 3rd Battalion Coldstream Guards. It is known that Thomas died after the armistice and was buried in Edingen Communal Cemetery in Belgium. The 'Soldiers who died in the Great War' database states he 'died' not he 'died of wounds' after the end of the war which makes it likely that he died of influenza. This pandemic flu killed an estimated 50 million people worldwide between June 1918 and December 1920.

During November and December 1918, the 3rd Coldstream Guards had travelled mostly by marching from Criel in France to Cologne in Germany according to their war diary.

1 November 1918	Criel	12 miles north east of Dieppe
15th	Cambrai	France
17th	Maubeuge	France
18th	Haulchin	France
19th	Anderlus	Belgium
20th	Charleroi	Belgium
24th	Fosse	Belgium
25th	Dave	Belgium
28th	Asseses	Belgium
5 December 1918	Miecret	Belgium
6th	Bomal	Belgium
7th	Jevigny	France
11th	Petit Their	France
12th	Moddersheid	crossed German frontier
13th	Underbreth	Germany
14th	Sotenich	Germany
15th	Kommern	Germany
16th	E.R.P.	Germany
17th	Epperen	Germany
18th	Cologne	Germany

The battalion stayed in Cologne and during January, 300 long service soldiers were despatched back to Britain. In February, the rest of the soldiers were gradually sent back to Britain for demobilisation.

The 'Soldiers who died in the Great War' database gives Thomas's death as the 11th February whereas the Commonwealth War Graves Commission states Thomas died between 11th November 1918 and 11th February 1919. Without records it is impossible to determine the circumstances of

Thomas's death. None of the other WWI soldiers buried in Edingen cemetery can be linked to dying at the same time as Thomas. They were:

Joseph Combes, Private 8986 died on the 25th December 1914, Sherwood Foresters (Notts. and Derby Regiment)

R Hornby, Rifleman 96409, died 28th October 1918, The King's (Liverpool) Regiment

Thomas Stobbs, Private 19415, died 11th November 1918, Coldstream Guards. *(N.B. On 11 November 1918, Thomas was still in France).*

H Wicks, Private 14505 died on the 22nd February 1919, 27th Suffolk Regiment

There are two possible explanations why Thomas was buried in Edingen.

Between the 19th November and the 5th December 1918, Thomas was marching through Belgium on route to Germany. The regiment was billeted in Charleroi - 40 miles from Edingen. Maybe Thomas became ill and was transferred to a hospital in this area and died in November or December.

The alternative is that Thomas reached Cologne with his battalion and in early February 1919, he was on his way back to Britain for demobilisation when he became ill and he died near Edingen and was buried here.

How sad for Thomas and his family. They all must have been relieved when the armistice was signed and were excited that the war had ended, and Thomas was out of danger. He would have been thankful that he had survived the horrors of war and along with his comrades would have been cheerful and happy. His death from illness was one of the many that would occur following the aftermath of war.

Thomas is remembered on the Witton le Wear Memorial.

A Smith

On the village war memorial is the name 'Private A Smith' serving with the Army Service Corps. Where do you start researching for 'A Smith'?

www.ancestry.co.uk identifies at least 2,986 men as 'A Smith' in the WWI military section. The Commonwealth War Graves Commission states there are 1350 'A Smiths' who died in WWI. Some would be false names of servicemen who did not want to be identified, but we can assume that our 'A Smith' was bona fide as his relatives put his name on the village memorial. There were 36 A Smith's who perished while serving in the Army Service Corps including soldiers from Consett, Fencehouses and Hetton le Hole, towns in County Durham. The records that are available for these men do not show any link to Witton le Wear or surrounding areas.

There were 27 'A Smiths' in the DLI, the county regiment, but again no obvious link. The nearest was Arthur Smith who came from Hunwick, four miles from Witton le Wear, and he is remembered on the Hunwick memorial so it is unlikely to be him. There is an Alfred Smith from Copley, seven miles from Witton le Wear, but he was a lance corporal with the Irish Rifles so again very unlikely to be our 'A Smith'.

In the 1911 census there was an Alfred Smith, a 25 year old gardener/domestic living at West Witton in the village, with the Bell family and he came from Ryhope so maybe...., just maybe......

In Flanders Field

In Flanders fields the poppies blow
Between the crosses, row on row
That mark our place; and in the sky
The larks, still bravely singing, fly
Scarce heard amid the guns below.

We are the Dead, short days ago
We lived, felt dawn, saw sunset glow,
Loved and were loved, and now we lie
In Flanders fields.

Take up your quarrel with the foe;
To you from failing hands we throw
The torch; be yours to hold it high.
If ye break faith with us you die
We shall not sleep, though poppies grow
In Flanders fields.

Dr. John McCrae
(A Canadian medical officer who served during the second battle of Ypres)

Prayers before battle. There was a common saying of the time saying that there were 'no athiests on a battlefield (or in a foxhole)'
(Author's collection)

German searchlights that were used all along the Western Front.
(Author's collection)

In Loving Memory of
JANE.
BELOVED WIFE OF THE LATE
WILLIAM SNAITH SANDERS,
DIED 5th FEB. 1938, AGED 78 YEARS.
ALSO OF JOHN THOMAS, SON OF THE ABOVE
REPORTED MISSING IN THE GREAT WAR
21st MARCH 1918. AGED 27 YEARS.

John Saunders remembered on his mother's gravestone in Witton le
Wear Cemetery.
(Author's collection)

Arras Memorial in France commemorates almost 35,000
Commonwealth dead with no known graves, who died in the Arras
sector between the spring of 1916 and August 1918, including
John Sanders. (CWGC)

Witton Park War Memorial with John Sanders name on the bottom line. (Author's collection)

North Eastern Railway War Memorial in York where Fred Hall and another 2235 employees of NER who died during WWI are remembered. (Author's collection)

Family grave of Kit
Whitton's family in
Witton le Wear cemetery.
(Author's collection)

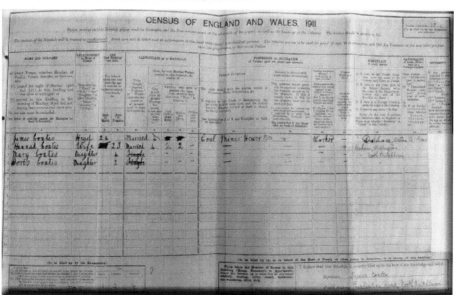

1911 census for James Coates and his family living in North Bitchburn.
(Author's collection)

Howden le Wear War
Memorial.
(Author's collection)

Close up of James Coates
name on Howden le
Wear War Memorial.
(Author's collection)

WHO FELL IN THE GREAT WAR.
1914-1918.

BELL.J. PTE. N.F.   HOOK.J. PTE. J.L.I.
BENNINGTON,O.PTE.WR.KAVANAGH,J. STK.R.N.
BROWELL,E. PTE. E.Y.   NUTLEY,J. PTE. N.F.
CLARK.G. SAP. R. E.   PARKIN,G. BDR.R.G.A.
CLARK. R.E.PTE. E.Y.   REID.F. PTE. D.L.I.
COATES.J. PTE. E.Y.   ROBINSON,J. PTE.R.N.I.
COOK.P. PTE. D.L.I.   SELL.G. PTE. D.L.I.
ECCLES.T. PTE.D.L.I.   SLEE.J.H. CPL. Y.R.
ETHERINGTON,D.TPR.HUS.TRIMBLE,H. PTE.D.L.I.
EVANS.T. SGT. D.F.   WALKER.F. PTE. D.L.I.
FOSTER.J.G. PTE.N.F.   WEARMOUTH,G.PTE.D.L.I
GIBSON,A. PTE. D.L.I.   WHITTON.W. PTE. D.L.I.
HARDY. S. PTE. N.F.   WILLSON.W. PTE. N.F.
HINDMOOR,G.PTE.D.L.I.WILLIAMS,E.PTE.K.R.R.
MOSES.J. PTE. E.Y.   WOOD.A. PTE. S.F.

Private George Walton Scott on home leave July 1918. The back of the photograph states it was taken by Thurlwell Ltd, Photographers Middlesboro, Darlington, West Hartlepool, Newcastle, Bishop Auckland and Gateshead and was probably taken in Bishop Auckland.
(Courtesy of the Scott Family)

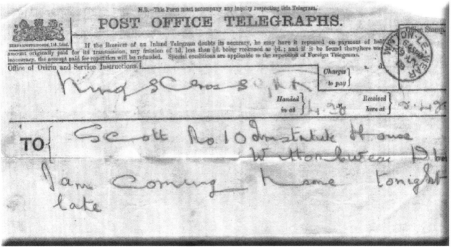

Telegram sent to Private Walton's family to tell them he was on his way home on leave on the 29th July 1918.
(Courtesy of the Scott Family)

Witton le Wear Railway Station where local lads would have caught the
train to take them away to war and also where they would come home
on leave or at the end of the war. A place of mixed emotions.
(Author's collection)

Private George Walton Scott's grave in
Wulverghem Lindenhoek Road Military
Cemetery.
(Author's collection)

The King commands me to assure you of the true sympathy of His Majesty and The Queen in your sorrow.

He whose loss you mourn died in the noblest of causes. His Country will be ever grateful to him for the sacrifice he has made for Freedom and Justice.

Secretary of State for War.

Letter sent on behalf of the King to George Scott's family after his death.
(Courtesy of the Scott Family)

Clock bought and treasured by George Scott's mother with money from Witton le Wear Welcome Home Fund.
(Courtesy of the Scott Family)

Administrative County of Durham

Civil Parish of ... Municipal Borough of ... Municipal Ward of ... Parliamentary Borough of Bishop Auckland Town of Bishop Auckland Rural Sanitary District of ... Urban Sanitary District of Bishop Auckland Ecclesiastical Parish of St Andrew

The undermentioned Houses are situate within the Boundaries of the

No. of Schedule	ROAD, STREET, &c, and No. or NAME of HOUSE	HOUSES (Inhabited)	HOUSES (Uninhabited)	HOUSES (Building)	NAME and Surname of each Person	RELATION to Head of Family	CONDITION as to Marriage	AGE (Males)	AGE (Females)	PROFESSION or OCCUPATION	Employer	Employed	Neither	WHERE BORN	Deaf-and-Dumb, Blind, Lunatic, Imbecile or Idiot
5	8 Newgate Street	1			Joseph Dean	Head	M	35		Grocer		x		Yorkshire Northallerton	
					Eliza	Wife	M		35					Lancashire Manchester	
					William	Son		12		Scholar				Durham Stockton	
					Arthur	Son				Scholar				Durham Bp Auckland	
					Albert	Son		7		Scholar				Durham Bp. A.	
					Ethel	Daur			4	Scholar				Durham Bp. A.	
6	6 Newgate Street	1			Arthur Hawburn	Head	M	34		Pharmaceutical Chemist	x			Durham Bishop Aⁿ	
					Mary	Wife	M		32					Durham Bishop Aⁿ	
					William Moor	Son	S	8		Scholar				Durham Bishop Aⁿ	
					Alice Charley	Servant	S		27	Genrl Servant Domestic		x		Durham Eldon	
					Patrick Craig	Head	M	38		Photographic Artist				Ireland	
					Mercy Elis	Wife	M		37	Draper				Durham Stockton	
					Mrs Arthur	Daur			4	Scholar				Dur. Bp. A.	
7	7 Newgate St	1			Robert Stevens	Son	S							Dur. Bp. A?	
8	21 Newgate Thos	1			Jane Ann Stevens	Servant				General Servant Domestic		H		Durham Scotland	
					William H. Kilburn	Head	M	41		Ironmonger		x		Dur. Bp Aⁿ	
					Matilda J. Kilburn	Wife	M		40					Peter's Island Norwich	
					Michel	Daur	S		10	Joiner?				Durham Bp. A?	
					Laura Helena Kidson	Visitor	S		36	Nurse - Domestic				Northumberland Newcastle	
					Eliz Ann Cleasly	Servant	S		20	Maid - Domestic				Durham Eldon	
					Mary Jane Oliver	Domestic	S		12	General Servant Domestic				Durham Longtide Spring	
9	4 Durham Chase	1	4		Arthur Heybourne	Head	M	54		Income Tax Collector		x		Durham Kirby Dirts	
					Mary Heybourne	Wife	M		14					Durham Fell Side	
					Annie Knoll	Daur			52	Scholar				Durham Cockfield	
					Ella	Sister	S							Dur. Kirby Dirts	
					Eliz Young	Servant	S		16	General Servant Domestic		x		Dur. Bp. Auck?	

1891 census for Newgate Street, Bishop Auckland. The Dean family are at the top but the page also shows the wide range of occupations of the residents of this part of Bishop Auckland. (Author's collection)

Front page of Albert Dean's attestation papers. The same papers were used for every serviceman.
(Crown Copyright - Author's collection)

Albert Dean's 'Statement of the Services' indicates the campaigns he served in, his unit and his promotions from February 1915 until September 1917 when he started training for a commission.
(Crown Copyright - Author's collection)

Albert Dean's Statement of the Services as a Commissioned Officer in May 1918.
(Crown Copyright - Author's collection)

A copy of the telegram sent on the 17th October 1918 to Albert Dean's mother informing her of his death in action.
(Crown Copyright - Author's collection)

Extract from the London Gazette on the 1 February 1919 when Albert was awarded the Military Cross.
(Crown Copyright - Author's collection)

Dean family gravestone in Witton le Wear Cemetery (Author's collection)

Albert Dean's name remembered on the family gravestone (Author's collection)

The midden cart at the top of Station Road c 1910 outside the Langstaff family homes. (Author's collection)

Administrative County	Durham																	

The undermentioned Houses are situate within the boundaries of the

No. of Schedule	ROAD, STREET, &c. and No. or NAME of HOUSE	HOUSES Inhabited			Name and Surname of each Person	RELATION to Head of Family	Condition as to Marriage	Age last Birthday of Males / Females	PROFESSION or OCCUPATION	Employer, Worker, or Own account	If Working at Home	WHERE BORN
63	Witton le Wear 1				George Langstaff	Head	Mar		Lime Dr Merchant	Employer		Durham Witton le Wear
					Mary A. Do	Wife	Mar					Do South Hetton
					Isabella Do	Daur		10				Do Witton le Wear
					Jane Do	Daur		7				Do do
					Henry Do	Son		5				Do do
					Bessie Do	Daur		1				Do do
64	Witton le Wear 1				Harry Langstaff	Head	Mar	36	Lime Dr Merchant	Employer		Do do
					Margaret Do	Wife	Mar	38				Do do
					Hannah Do	Daur		9				Do do
					Isabella Do	Daur		7				Do do
					John Do	Son		5				Do do
					Richard Do	Son		2				Do do
					William Do	Son		4/12				Do do

1901 census for the Langstaff family in Station Road, Witton le Wear. Harry and his family lived in Laburnum House at Number 17 and his cousin Richard and family lived across the road at Number 16. (Author's collection)

Private Harry Langstaff
(Courtesy of Wolsingham School)

Langstaff Family c 1915. It is possible that the young man in the soldier's cap was Harry or another local lad.
(Witton le Wear History Group collection)

Example of a death plaque that was sent to the families of all servicemen who died during WWI.
(Author's collection)

The three most common medals awarded to British servicemen during
WW1. The 1914/15 Star, the British Medal and the Victory Medal.
(Author's collection)

Dr John Dodds, the local doctor outside the Victoria Hotel.
(Witton le Wear History Group collection)

Witton le Wear Methodist Chapel
(Author's collection)

Employees of Langstaff's sawmills c1910
(Witton le Wear History Group collection)

The Towers. Home of the Henry Stobart who provided local employment
and whose son John served in the Royal Field Artillery during WW1.
(Author's collection)

Private Walter Gillard
(top right) with three
DLI comrades serving
in France
(courtesy of Gillard
Brothers)

Private Walter Gillard
taken on the
20th August 1916 near
Wasley, Somme area
(courtesy of Gillard
Brothers)

Wolsingham School Memorial Oak Trees
(Author's collection)

The plaque beside the Memorial Oaks
(Author's collection)

The men who served and survived

As the result of an Act of Parliament passed on 6th February 1918, servicemen over the age of 21 became eligible to vote in their home constituency. The first so-called Absentee Voters List was published nationally on 15th October 1918 and it is thought that it was compiled from details supplied by the men. This would not explain the discrepancies of regimental information so the information may have been supplied by families on their behalf. It also does not explain that many of the soldiers named on the list were under the age of 21 in October 1918. The Absentee Voters 1918 list for the parish of Witton le Wear is held by the Durham County Record Office and 53 men are listed. The following information has been obtained about these men using the Absentee Voters List 1918, the 1881, 1891, 1901 and 1911 census, WWI medal rolls and service records where available and information from the graves database of Witton le Wear Cemetery. It is as accurate as possible but any further information would be very acceptable.

Thomas William Allinson, 12th West Yorkshire Regiment

Thomas lived at Hill House Farm and was serving as a Private with the 12th West Yorkshire Regiment. The voters list gives his number as 45141 but this is an error rectified in his medal roll card. He also served with the Army Labour Corps and had a second regimental number of 631294. In 1911, Thomas was living at home with his parents Thomas and Hannah, and his four sisters, Elsie, Edith, Emily and Norah. In 1918 he must just have been 21 years old and eligible to vote for the first time. Thomas received the British and the Victory medals at the end of the War. There are five Allinson graves in the village cemetery without headstones which could belong to this family. Norah is certainly buried there when she died in 1989 aged 88 years and has a headstone in place.

Joseph Edward Armstrong, West Yorkshire Regiment

Joseph Armstrong was the oldest son of William and Emma Armstrong and in 1911 he lived at 14 Cemetery Bank with his parents and his sister Florence. He served with the West Yorkshire Regiment and also the Army Labour Corp. Joseph was eligible for the British and the Victory medals at the end of the War. There are three Armstrong graves in the village cemetery without headstones which could belong to this family.

Thomas Allinson and Joseph were of similar ages and probably enlisted together and stayed in the same regiments throughout their army service. There are no surviving army records for either man.

Thomas Bainbridge, 9th Border Regiment
John Bainbridge, 4th Durham Light Infantry
Robert Bainbridge, 4th Durham Light Infantry

Thomas was the youngest son of Elizabeth Bainbridge and his father died between 1897 and 1901. In 1901, Thomas aged 3 years, was living at Thompson Street, Witton Park with his mother, Elizabeth, his older sister Mary aged 24 years, and his brother John aged 7 years. In the 1911 census, Thomas, aged 13 was living at West Witton, Witton le Wear with his mother, brother William aged 17 and a boarder, a widower

Samuel Drake. Thomas was the youngest child of the family and possibly his sister Mary was the eldest. There was a 21 year age gap between the siblings and although no record can be found to prove this, it is highly likely that Robert was also an older brother. John, as the 1901 census shows is a brother as well.

Thomas volunteered and served with the 9th Border Regiment early in 1915. He went to France on the 7th September 1915 which gave him entitlement to the 1914/15 Star and he also was awarded the British and Victory medal. When he was discharged from active service on 6th April 1919, his home address was 31 Station Road, Witton le Wear.

According to the Absentee Voters List, his brothers John and Robert also lived at the same address. John served with the 4th Durham Light Infantry and Robert was a Private with the 5th Reserve Durham Light Infantry and both enlisted after Thomas. All of them survived the war and unfortunately there are no surviving army records for any of the brothers.

There are 4 unmarked Bainbridge graves in the village cemetery which may be related to this family.

Robert Roland Brooksbank, 5th Durham Light Infantry

Robert was born in the Auckland area in January 1898 but was not living in Witton le Wear at the time of the 1911 census. According to the Absentee Voters List in 1918, his home address was 5 Cemetery Road, Witton le Wear. Robert served with the 5th reserve Durham Light Infantry and was discharged at the end of the war. He later married Emily Ann and he and

Emily are buried in the village cemetery. Robert died in June 1966 at the age of 68 and Emily died May 1980 aged 82 years.

Stephen Binks, 4th Yorkshire Regiment

Stephen was a farm labourer who was married to Ellen Binks and lived at Carr's Terrace, although the Absentee Voters List gives his home address as 21 West End. He enlisted in the 4th Yorkshire Regiment. At the end of the war Stephen was entitled to the British and Victory medals. There is one unmarked grave in the cemetery linked to the Binks family.

Albert Brown, 9th Border Regiment
Frederick Brown, 9th Border Regiment

Albert and Frederick were sons of Abraham and Elizabeth Brown. In 1911, they lived in Station Road with their parents and their brother Ralph and sisters Annie and Esther. Albert was the older brother and listed as a pony driver in a stone mine, Frederick was five years younger and still at school in 1911.

Albert enlisted into the 9th Border Regiment in September 1914 and went to France in September 1915. He also served in Macedonia and met up with Joe Jackson in Salonika. Albert survived the war and was awarded the 1914/15 Star, British and Victory medals and was demobilized from active service on the 7th March 1919. His home address was 7 Station Road.

Fred also served a very similar army career with the 9th Border Regiment and probably enlisted alongside Albert as their career was the comparable apart from Fred's demobilization on the 21st February 1919, two weeks before his brother. Fred's address at demobilisation was 11 Post Office Street.

Joseph Brown, Royal Army Medical Corps

Joseph lived at 12 Station Road in 1918 and served during WWI as Staff Sergeant in the 8th Company of the Royal Army Medical Corps. He previously served with the Northumberland Fusiliers. He was born in May 1879, married Sarah and both were buried in the village cemetery. Joseph died in 1957 and Sarah died in 1959. His regimental number was recorded incorrectly in the Absentee Voters List.

Stephen Carr, Royal Engineers

Stephen originally enlisted in the Coldstream Guards and then transferred to the Royal Engineers where he was a Sapper with the 33rd Light Rail Company. In 1918, his address was 10 Low Row, North Bitchburn.

Edmund Coates, Royal Engineers

Edmund was a Witton le Wear man, born and bred. He was born on the 30th October 1888, the son of George and Mary Coates. Edmund was named after his grandfather who died in 1887 just before Edmund was born. He had one sister Margaret. In the 1911 census Edmund was employed as a joiner. His army records are one of only 40% that survive. Edmund enlisted with the Royal Engineers in 1915 at the age of 27 years and 40 days. His home address was 18 High Street, Witton le Wear. Edmund was 5ft 7½ inches tall, weighed 144 lbs., had a 38 inch chest and a lung expansion of 3 inches. He was classed fit for army service although he was slightly flat footed. Edmund was mobilized in March 1916 and posted to 73rd Company. He was wounded on the 22nd July 1917 and retrained as a wheelwright and was promoted to lance corporal. On the 1st March 1919, Edmund disobeyed an order and was deprived of his stripes and suffered close arrest for 3 days. In April, he moved to 226th Company and was demobilized in September 1919. Edmund's parents are buried in the village cemetery and when Edmund died on the 2nd March 1967 he was also buried there.

Ralph Henry Carr, 2nd Coldstream Guards

Ralph enlisted and rose to the rank of lance corporal with the 2nd Coldstream Guards. No other information is known about Ralph except that he lived in North Bitchburn.

John Darbyshire, Royal Engineers
Benjamin Darbyshire, Royal Field Artillery

The Darbyshire family lived at Witton Freestone Quarry where John Darbyshire senior, was manager. In 1911, his son John Ralph was a quarryman aged 32 and was living at home. There also was Benjamin, John senior's grandson. Benjamin may have been John Ralph's son or his nephew. Also living at the quarry was John senior's wife Margaret, sons Tom and William, daughter Jemima and grandchildren Edward and Mildred.

John Ralph served with the Royal Engineers Inland Waterways and Drainage. Benjamin served with the Royal Field Artillery as a gunner. Both survived the war and there is a family grave in the cemetery with the following inscription.

"In loving memory of John and Margaret Darbyshire and all members of their family laid to rest in this cemetery from January 2nd 1918 Remembered by their grandchildren"

Walter Gillard

Walter Gillard was born in London in January 1879 and had an older brother George. For some unknown reason, the children were brought up by their Aunt and Uncle in Croft, Yorkshire where Uncle William Dawson was a groom to the Chaytor family at Croft Hall. By 1901, the family were living at South Parade, Croft with Ellen and William. George was employed as a domestic groom, and Walter was a valet to the Chaytor family.

Around 1903, Walter married his wife Elizabeth who had also been in service as a housekeeper to the Chaytors. Their daughter Lillian was born around 1904 and son Walter was born in 1911. In July 1913, Sir William Chaytor died and the hereditary title passed to his younger brother Sir Edmund Chaytor of Witton Castle. Walter and his family moved to Witton Castle where he became his lordship's valet.

Typical of many men in the area, Walter joined the Durham Light Infantry Territorial Army at Bishop Auckland and when war broke out he transferred into the regular army and served with the 6th Durhams. His army records have not survived but there are records about Walter's discharge following injuries in 1916/1917 for which he received a weekly war pension of 13 shillings and 9 pence. The records are not specific to what the injuries were, but they were 'aggravated by active service conditions'. His grandsons Clive and George Gillard, who still live in Witton le Wear, remember hearing that he had suffered from exposure to gas.

In September 1917, Walter was discharged from the army into the 5th (reserve) Battalion of the DLI and he returned to the family home in Witton le Wear. In 1916, Sir Edmund had taken a commission with the Scots Guards and Witton Castle was closed down retaining only a skeleton staff. Lady Isobel Chaytor and her three children left the castle on 4th August in a special saloon carriage to live at Putney, London. Elizabeth Gillard and her family moved to 3 School Street in Witton le Wear, the house to which Walter returned at the end of the war. Walter received the British Medal and the Victory Medal which are still in the family's possession. After the war, Walter and Mary moved to Wear Valley Junction where they remained for the rest of their lives. Walter returned to Witton Castle as Sir Edmund's valet when the family came back to the area. Walter became a well-known local cricketer playing for Witton le Wear Cricket Club and died in 1942.

William Oliver Henderson, Royal Engineers

Nineteen pages of William's army records are accessible, but they are not very clear. He lived at 12 High Street and enlisted on the 2nd March 1916, one of the first conscripted recruits, but was not called to active service until June 1917, when posted to the Inland Water Transport Section of the Royal Engineers at the age of 23 years and 5 months. He had been born in 1894 but was not living in Witton le Wear in 1911. His mother Margaret was his next of kin and William was taller than average at 5ft 11 inches.

William sailed from Hull on the 2nd August 1917 and landed in Basrah in Mesopotamia (present day Iraq) on the 9th December 1917. Prior to enlistment he appears to have been a seaman. He was acting corporal from September – November 1918 when he was second in command of Class III vessels, reverted to being a sapper and then in October 1919 he was appointed acting sergeant. William left Basrah on the 8th January 1920 for demobilisation and this was effective from 18th March 1920. After he came out of the Royal Engineers, William applied for his First Mate certificate to allow him to continue working at sea. He received his British and Victory medals in September 1922.

Benjamin Metcalfe Heslop, West Yorkshire Regiment

Benjamin was born in January 1890 in Witton le Wear. His parents were George and Mary Anna and he had one sister Dinah who was three years younger. In the 1911 census, the family were living at 2 Railway Terrace and both Benjamin and his father were coal miners. Benjamin enlisted and served with the West Yorkshire Regiment and after demobilisation he married Frances. Benjamin died on the 7th July 1961 aged 71 years and Frances died on the 14th March 1979 aged 82 years. Both are buried in Witton le Wear Cemetery.

Edward Heslop (Ted), 5th Border Regiment

The Heslop family lived in South View, Witton le Wear. In 1911, the head of household was Christopher, with his wife Mary Ann, and their daughters: Martha, Rebecca and Dinah. According to the census, Christopher and Mary Ann had another two children who were not living at home. One of these would have been Ted. He served as a Lance Corporal in the 5th Border Regiment and in 1916 Ted was posted to Malta from where he sent his parents regular postcards.[25] He was later transferred to the Western Front, where he was wounded in the left elbow by shrapnel on the 3rd October 1918[26]. The shrapnel was extracted in hospital in France and Ted recovered and returned home to 25 Station Road, Witton le Wear.

Henry Heslop, Lieutenant: 6th Northumberland Fusiliers

Henry was born in Witton le Wear on 13th July 1892 and in 1911 he was living with his parents George and Isabella at Pear Tree House, Witton le Wear. He attended Woodhouse Grove School, Apperley Bridge, near Bradford which was a boarding school run for Methodists. Henry was later employed as an articled clerk in a chartered accountant's office and his father was a colliery agent and secretary.

Henry's army records were obtained from the National Archives and are very informative. He enlisted at Newcastle upon Tyne in December 1915 and was 5ft 9½ inches tall. He weighed 147 lbs. his chest measurement was 37 inches and he passed his medical as being very healthy. Henry reported for basic training to Helmsley on 6th December and joined the 21st

---

[25] Auckland Chronicle, 3rd August 1916
[26] Auckland Chronicle, 17th October 1918

Territorial Battalion of the Kings Royal Rifles. By the end of January he had been promoted to unpaid Lance Corporal and on 5th May he joined the British Expeditionary Force in France. He must have showed leadership qualities as on 22nd November he was discharged from the Kings Royal Rifles and started training for a temporary commission. He had been selected for his commission training to start in July 1916, but as he was serving overseas, this was postponed to the next available course. It was Henry's wish to be appointed to the 2nd/6th Northumberland Fusiliers when he passed out. On the application form for his commission he stated he was able to ride "a little". His character reference was provided by Henry James Stobart from Witton Towers, who had known Henry for 10 years. His other reference was provided by Lt Colonel Edward Robinson of the Royal Engineers (territorial) who had known Henry for 5 years. As Henry had never any previous army service, this must have been a family friend or acquaintance. His headmaster from Woodhouse Grove School also gave an educational reference.

Henry graduated as a 2nd Lieutenant on the 23rd November 1916 and was posted to the 6th Northumberland Fusiliers[27]. He was promoted to Lieutenant on the 23rd May 1918[28]. The Army lists have him serving with the 6th Northumberland Fusiliers in October 1918 whereas the Absentee Voters List have Henry serving with the 2/6th Durham Light Infantry. Whichever fighting force he was with he would have seen some very heavy fighting in the Western Front and would have led his men into battle on many occasions.

Henry survived the war and the final page of his army records state that he enrolled in the Officers Emergency

---

[27] Army List May 1918. ref 941
[28] Army List Oct 1918. Ref 940c

Reserve on the 1st October 1938 and he would be removed from this list in July 1947. Whether he served during World War II in unknown but requires further research and will be included in the future book covering 1939 – 1945.

Anthony Jackson, 3rd Coldstream Guards
Joe Jackson, Army Cyclist Corps
Thomas Jackson, 18th Yorkshire Regiment

Anthony (called Anty), Joe and Thomas were brothers who lived at 9 Railway Terrace. Joe's diary and his story is described earlier in the book. In 1911, they were living with their parents, Anty and Mary Ann, sisters, Edith, Barbara, Dora and brother Alexander. Three older siblings, Elizabeth, Daisy May and Florence were not living at home.

Anty had been a school teacher prior to the war but after enlistment he fought with the 3rd Battalion of the Coldstream Guards and served alongside Thomas Stobbs from Wear Terrace. After the war, Anty returned to the village and eventually ran the family market garden business at the back of Railway Terrace. He died on the 27th November 1975 and was buried in the village cemetery.

Thomas was born in 1896 in Witton le Wear and by 1911 he was a 15 year old grocer's errand boy. He attested in the army on the 15th December 1915 one month before his 20th birthday. He was immediately posted to the Army Reserve and was eventually mobilized on the 30th April 1918. He was initially assigned to the Northumberland Fusiliers, but in June was transferred to the 18th Battalion of the Yorkshire Regiment. Thomas only served in England and was discharged as surplus to military requirements on the 22nd January 1919 and was given a gratuity of £25. Thomas followed his brother Joe to America in December 1921.

George Jamieson (Jimmeson), 3rd Manchester Regiment

George's surname is Jimmeson in the Absentee Voters List but Jamieson in the Army Medal Roll. He lived at 8 School Street and served as a Private with the 3rd Manchester Regiment. Little else is known about George as he was not identified in the 1911 census and his army records are not available. He did not enlist until after 1915 therefore was probably a conscripted soldier. George did survive the war and was entitled to the British and Victory medals.

Harry Langstaff, Durham Light Infantry

Harry was listed in the Absentee Voters List of 1918 with a home address of Laburnum House, 17 Station Road, Witton le Wear, but he died before the end of October 1918 and is buried in Rouen, France. His story is found earlier in this book.

Richard Langstaff, East Yorkshire Regiment and the Lincoln Regiment

In 1911, Richard was living at 16 Station Road, Witton le Wear with his father Henry, mother Margaret (nee Brownbridge), sisters Hannah and Isabella and brother's John and William. Everyone in the family had been born in the village. Richard enlisted in April 1917, served with the East Yorkshire Regiment and also the Lincoln Regiment. There are no military records for Richard apart from his medal roll card which has his name wrongly recorded as Longstaff. Richard was wounded in August 1918 and had to have his leg amputated, like his cousin Harry Langstaff. He sent a field card to his parents saying he had been wounded and was in hospital but quite well.[29] Thankfully Richard survived and returned to Witton le Wear.

John Cecil Lowson, Durham Light Infantry and 9th West Riding Regiment

John's army records are accessible, but of poor legibility. He was born in Evenwood Parish and was living at Marshall Green Farm when he enlisted in the Durham Light Infantry Reserve in December 1915. He had married Mary Ann Simpson on February 25th 1912, and had a daughter called Lettice Lowson born in November 1913. John was a farmer and a colliery owner.

John was sent to France in August 1916 with the 9th West Riding Regiment, but in November he suffered with trench foot, was admitted to hospital and sailed back to the UK on hospital ship 'S.S. Aberdonian'. In April 1917, he went back to France and in December returned home to the base depot after suffering the effects of being gassed. In September 1918 he returned to France for a third time with the 3rd Battalion Durham Light Infantry but suffered gunshot wounds to both legs on the 4th November 1918. He was taken to hospital and was transferred to Halifax on the 9th November. His conduct sheet also showed that he had one episode on 29th November when stationed in Halifax, where he was absent without leave from

---

[29] Auckland Chronicle, 5th September 1918

124

tattoo and was given 120 hours detention as a punishment. On the 21st January 1919, John left the army but signed the Statement as to Disability form that he had no disability due to his military service. This leads you to think that his injuries were of a minor degree. He returned to live at 14 West End with Mary and his daughter.

George Harrison Laverick, Royal Garrison Artillery

The 1911 census showed George, aged 28 and single, living at 4 Cemetery Road with his father John, and his sisters Margaret and Jane. His mother had died prior to 1911. George was a mason's labourer who worked for the Railway Company. He enlisted in the Royal Garrison Artillery and became a gunner with the 265th Siege Battalion serving in France. At the end of the war he was awarded the Victory and British Medals. There is an unmarked Laverick grave in the village cemetery which may contain the remains of a member of this family.

Robert Laverick, 6th West Yorkshire Regiment

In 1911, Robert was a 13 year old schoolboy (born April 1897) who lived at 19 Post Office Street with his widowed mother Emily, his older brother Alfred, and his two older sisters, Alvina and Margaret. Robert enlisted in the 6th West Yorkshire Regiment and was discharged into the army reserve on the 12th February 1919 at the age of 21. In the village cemetery is the grave of Robert's mother Emily. The inscription reads:

'In loving memory of Emily Laverick died 26th August 1925 aged 67 years, darling mother of Eliza, Hannah, Sarah, Alfred, Alvina, Margaret, Robert'

William Marr, Durham Light Infantry and Machine Gun Corp

There is no record of William living in Witton le Wear in 1911, but he did live at 7 West End when he enlisted in the Durham Light Infantry in May 1915. He quickly transferred to the Machine Gun Corp where he rose to the rank of Sergeant. William was awarded the 1914/15 Star, the Victory and the British Medals. There are five unmarked graves assigned to the Marr Family in the cemetery.

Robert Moreland, 18th Durham Light Infantry

Robert was born at the Plumpton estate, near Harrogate in 1880 and had married Ethel in 1900. They had three children, Evelyn, John and Robert and in 1911, were living at 17 West End. Both John (c1903) and Robert (c1905) were born in Witton le Wear. Robert senior was a domestic poultryman and was conscripted into the Durham Light Infantry. He rose to the rank of Acting Corporal before he was discharged in 1919. The 18th DLI served in France from March 1916 until the end of the war. Robert was awarded the Victory and British medals. Ethel died in 1947 and Robert lived until 1971 when he died at the age of 91. They are both buried in the village cemetery.

John Oddy, 28th Royal Fusiliers

The Oddy family have a long standing tradition of living in Witton le Wear. In 1911, John was an 18 year old lawyer's clerk living with his mother, Amelia, a widow and his sister Jane Watson. Jane had a 2 year old son called Freddy Oddy. The family lived at 2 Cemetery Road and his grandparents lived next door. John joined the 28th Royal Fusiliers and rose to the rank of Sergeant. As a lance corporal in July 1916, John returned home to Witton le Wear prior to deployment to the Western Front. He left with expressions of 'God speed and a safe return' from a host of friends and family.[30] John survived the war and returned to the village.

George Peacock, Lance Sergeant 9th Border Regiment

George Peacock was born at Nidderdale, Yorkshire and was the eldest son of Mary and John Peacock. John was a lead miner and when work in the lead mining industry ceased sometime between 1905 and 1911, the family moved from Fountains Earth St Chads in the West Riding of Yorkshire to 8 Railway Terrace, Witton le Wear. In 1911, John's mother Margaret Peacock also lived with them and the census shows that George had 2 sisters, Emily age 11 and Miriam age 6, and 2 brothers Sydney aged 10 and William aged 8. Three other daughters were born after 1911, Lily, May and Mary.

George enlisted in the 9th Border Regiment in September 1914 and by the 7th September 1915, he was serving in France. George sailed with the regiment to Salonika in late 1915 where he fought in the northern trenches. On several occasions George met up with neighbour Joe Jackson while in Greece. George was promoted to Corporal and then Lance Sergeant and was demobilised on the 7th March 1919.

George returned to Witton le Wear and married Annie Jane Brown. They were both buried in the village cemetery. George died on the 15th August 1960 and Annie died on the 5th January 1980 at the age of 82 years.

---

[30] Auckland Chronicle, 27th July 1916

John Potts, Royal Garrison Artillery

John Potts was born in Witton le Wear around 1895. His parents Walter and Sarah had 8 children, two of whom died at an early age. In 1911, the family were living at 9 School Street, the children being Annie aged 18, John aged 16, Esther aged 14 and Bertha aged 11. The two other siblings were away from home. John like his father was a brickyard labourer. John became a gunner and driver in the Heavy Artillery Battalion of the Royal Garrison Artillery. He returned home after the war and was awarded the Victory and British Medals. There are nine unmarked graves in the cemetery attributed to the Potts Family.

Thomas Potts, Border Regiment and 23rd Northumberland Fusiliers

Three houses up from John Potts lived Thomas and his family and it is not known whether Thomas was related to John. In 1911, Thomas's mother Hannah who had been widowed and remarried in 1895, was living with her husband William Barker, a tailor in 12 School Street, Witton le Wear. At this time, Thomas was a 31 year old widower who worked as a colliery labourer. Also in the house were two children Gladys aged 6 and Raymond aged 1 and it is very likely that they were Thomas's children. His sister Emma Jane, a 36 year old spinster also lived in the house and was employed as a dressmaker.

Thomas had been born in Witton le Wear, moved to Brandon for work but returned to the village before Raymond was born. He enlisted in the army early in 1915 and served in France from 3rd September 1915 with the Border Regiment and later in Salonika. In 1916 he was posted to Maidstone in Kent where he met and married again. Unfortunately this marriage did not last long as his wife died of influenza in early December 1918 at the age of 26[31]. Thomas later transferred to the Northumberland Fusiliers and was promoted to Sergeant. Whether he returned to Witton le Wear is not known but he was awarded the 1914/15 Star, the Victory and British medals. There are nine unmarked graves in the cemetery attributed to the Potts Family.

Frederick Proud, Royal Garrison Artillery

Little is known about Frederick Proud. He lived at 26 Station Road, Witton le Wear and served as a gunner with the 136 Siege Battalion of the Royal Garrison Artillery. Frederick was awarded the Victory and British Medals after the war. He was not living in the village in 1911 and there are no graves in the cemetery to link with this family.

Joseph Proud, West Yorkshire Regiment and Agricultural Company Labour Corp

The Proud Family lived at Poplar House, 9 Station Road, Witton le Wear. In 1911, Joseph aged 26 and his brother Ralph aged 43 were both stone masons. Their sister Mary Elizabeth was 33 and had no recorded employment. Also living at this address was their mother Mary, a widow aged 64 years.

Joseph most probably was conscripted into the West Yorkshire Regiment and transferred to an Agricultural Labour Company which was part of the Army Labour Corp. The Labour

---

[31] Auckland Chronicle, 12 December 1918

Corp was often manned by soldiers of low medical grade. Most were soldiers who had been wounded, suffered sickness or injury and were employed on farms. The agricultural industry had lost a very high proportion of its men to the services and this was a way to provide manpower. His army service was probably in the UK somewhere as there is no evidence of him serving overseas, but Joseph survived the war. It is not known where Joseph lived after he came out of the armed services.

The family link to the village was strong as Joseph's sister Mary who died on the 26th November 1918 was buried in the village cemetery along with brothers Henry, who died 6th May 1929 and Ralph who died 18 September 1931.

Geoffrey Purson, 48th Infantry Brigade

No census or war records have been found about Geoffrey Purson from Witton le Wear. In the 1918 Absentee Voters List his address was Witton House and he served as a Captain in the 48th Infantry Brigade which was made up mostly of Irish Regiments but from 1916 – 1918 included the 48th Machine Gun Corps and a regiment from the Northumberland Fusiliers. This was possibly Geoffrey's link to the 48th Infantry Brigade. They were involved in very heavy fighting in the Battles of the Somme 1916 and 1918 and on the Ypres Salient where they suffered very heavy losses in the spring offensive of 1918.

John Richards, Royal Garrison Artillery
Robert Richards, 8th Durham Light Infantry

John and Robert were brothers who lived at the Victoria Hotel in Witton le Wear. They did not live in the village in 1911 and both were probably conscripted.   Little is known about John, but Robert was taken prisoner and the Red Cross Society sent the family a postcard informing them of this but saying 'he is quite well'.[32] Both men survived the war and were awarded British and Victory Medals.   There is an unmarked grave in the cemetery for Richards but it is not known if this is linked to the family.   No army records survive for either brother.

Herbert Roper, Military Foot Police

Herbert was the youngest child of James and Jane Roper and was born at Coniscliffe, Yorkshire in November 1884. During 1891, the family lived at Scruton, near Bedale, and in 1901 they were living at Loftus.   His father James and brother Henry were gamekeepers, and his brother Albert became a market gardener. He also had an older sister Jennie.

In 1911, Herbert's parents were living in Witton Towers, Witton le Wear along with their son Albert who was by then 27 years old, serving the Stobart family.   Herbert had married Margaret Carr from Durham City, on the 25th April 1908 by 1911 they a one year old daughter called Dora.   He was employed as a gardener and domestic help and they lived in Rose Cottage, Eggleston in Teesdale. They later had two more children born in South Shields, Joan on 8th August 1911 and James on the 11th September 1913.

---

[32] Auckland Chronicle, 31st October 1918

Herbert changed jobs and from 1914 he worked for the North East Railway Police, living at Cleadon. He attested for Army Reserve on 10th December 1915 at South Shields, but was not called into service until 7th August 1916 when he was accepted to join the Military Foot Police and immediately appointed Lance Corporal. His medical prior to acceptance in the Military Foot Police showed that he had bunions (hallux valgus) on both feet and to ensure he was fit for service he had to have a week's trial on the drill square to ensure his feet could take the pace.

The Military Foot Police was formed in 1885 and it served along with the Military Mounted Police. After World War I they amalgamated to become the Corp of Military Police and after service in World War II, they became the Corp of Royal Military Police in 1946.

Herbert went to France on the 12th April 1917 sailing from Southampton and arrived in Rouen four days later. He spent the next 2 years in the Abbeville area apart from 2 periods of home leave from 7th January 1918 until 21st January 1918 and 25th November 1918 until 9th December 1918. On the 22nd July 1918, Herbert became ill with influenza and was hospitalised for 8 days. Luckily he regained his heath and returned to active service with his unit. Herbert finally returned to the UK on the 6th May 1919 and was demobilised on the 21st August 1919 to his home at Quarry Head, Toft Hill, County Durham.

Why he is listed on the Witton le Wear Absentee Voters List in unclear? At some time prior to his marriage he must have lived in the village and probably never changed his name on the voters list as he was constantly moving around the North East.

Charles Robson, 19th Lancashire Fusiliers

There is little information about Charles apart from his home address being 7 Wear Terrace in the Absentee Voters List of 1918. He served with the 19th Lancashire Fusiliers and survived the war.

William Rutter, 8th East Yorkshire Regiment
Arthur Rutter, 9th Border Regiment

Brothers William and Arthur Rutter lived with their parents at the Gate House of Witton Castle. William was only a year older than Arthur and no doubt the boys were very close. In 1911, William, aged 18, was working as a groom and Arthur aged 17, was a miner. They also had an older sister, Mary Jane and the three siblings had all been born in Crook, County Durham. Their father William was a coachman on the Castle estate.

The brothers enlisted together in September 1914 and were both sent to France two days apart in September 1915. William was serving with the East Yorkshire Regiment and was eventually promoted to Sergeant. Arthur served with the 9th Border Regiment and served in the Western Front and Salonika, He was demobilised into the Army Reserve on the 25th March 1919. Both boys were awarded the 1914/15 Star, the Victory and the British Medals. William and Arthur would have shared many tales after the war.

There are 2 unmarked Rutter graves in the village cemetery, but it is unclear if they are linked to the family.

George Walton Scott, South Lancashire Regiment

By the time the Absentee Votes list was produced in October 1918, George Walton Scott had perished on the battlefields south of Ypres on the 25th September 1918. His story is told earlier in this book.

Henry Stephenson, Royal Garrison Artillery

Henry lived at 21 Station Road, Witton le Wear and served in the 181st Heavy Battalion of the Royal Garrison Artillery. There is 1 unmarked Stephenson grave in the cemetery.

John William Stobart, Lieutenant with the Royal Field Artillery

John born in 1898 was the eldest son of Henry Gervas Stobart who was the owner of sawmills and collieries and the employer of many of the young men who went off to war. The family lived at Witton Towers and in the 1911 census, there were 17 people living in the house, Henry and his Canadian wife Bessie, daughters Jean, Ruth, Lettice and Sheila, son Anthony, nine servants and a boarder. John was not present but possibly at boarding school.

John joined the Regular Army and passed out as a 2nd Lieutenant on the 26th May 1916[33]. He went to France on 1st July 1916. He served with the 179th Army Brigade, Royal Field Artillery and was promoted to Lieutenant in November 1917[34]. No records survive for John during his war service apart from

---

[33] Army List July 1916 Ref 537h
[34] Army List September 1918 Ref. 533b

his medal roll card. John was discharged from active service and went to live at Bedale Hall, Bedale in North Yorkshire.

Thomas Stobbs, Coldstream Guards
John Stobbs, 15th Durham Light Infantry
Joseph Stobbs, 18th Durham Light Infantry

Thomas Stobbs is mentioned previously in this book and he died during February 1919 in Belgium.

He had two younger brothers who also served overseas, John and Joseph. The family lived at Grey Mare House, 6 West End, Witton le Wear. John was born 1893, and Joseph was born in 1896. The three boys would have been swept up in the fervour for war and all enlisted early in the conflict.

John fought with the 15th Durham Light Infantry and travelled to France on the 11th September 1915. In July 1916, he was injured and wrote home to his mother telling her that he had been taken to the base hospital and then to Southport via Southampton. He wrote "I have got a little shrapnel bullet in my right arm, and have been under X-rays, and the bullet has been located and found on the extreme of my right breast. It will not be a serious matter to remove it when the time comes. I am quite happy where we are now."[35] It is not known if he returned to the Western Front.

Joseph was also with the Durham Light Infantry but served with the 18th Battalion and went to Egypt in December 1915. He would have served alongside Alec Richardson, mentioned previously and who was later to die on the Western Front, but the Egyptian experience was a fairly pleasant

---
[35] Auckland Chronicle, 20 July 1916

experience. Joseph would have travelled to France in 1916, but it is unknown if the three brothers met up at any time. The boys survived the fighting and saw the armistice and probably thought they would all soon be home in Witton le Wear. Little were they to know that Thomas would die before he reached home. All three were awarded 1914/15 Stars, the Victory Medals and the British Medals.

Jack Todd, 9th Border Regiment

Jack lived at 5 High Street, Witton le Wear and served from September 1914 in the Border Regiment. He went to France on the 7th September 1915, fought in Macedonia and was discharged into the army reserve on 7th March 1919. There is one Todd unmarked grave in the cemetery but it is unknown if it is linked to this family.

George Robert Vasey, Army Service Corps

George lived at 20 West End, Witton le Wear and he served with the Army Service Corps at a base depot. At its peak during WWI the Army Service Corps had over 10,000 officers and over 315,000 men. The main responsibility of the Army Service Corps was the movement of all supplies required by the army, including ammunition, clothing, equipment, food and fuel. During the war, supplies were moved by horse-drawn, steam and motor powered vehicles as well as by rail and waterways.

It is difficult to visualise the complexity of keeping the army supplied and the following statistics may give a basic understanding.

	Size of forces on Western Front		Monthly issues in lbs (Pounds weight) or Gallons			
	Men	Horses	Meat	Bread	Forage	Petrol (Galls)
1914 August	120,000	53,000	3,600,000	4,500,000	5,900,000	842,000
1918 November	3,000,000	500,000	67,500,000	90,000,000	32,250,000	13,000,000

('The Long Long Trail' http://www.1914-1918.net/)

George served with the Army Remounts Service which was responsible for the supply of trained horses and the above table shows the numbers involved. Almost all front line services relied on horses whether they were for cavalry divisions, field ambulances, artillery or for the cookhouses and communication. The efficiency required to keep the supply of horses cannot be underestimated.

George was demobilised in 1919 and probably came back to Witton le Wear.

Thomas Ward, Royal Defence Corps

In 1918, Thomas's home address was 11 Wear Terrace and he served with the 200th Reserve Company of the Royal Defence Corps that covered the Northern Region. The Royal Defence Corps was formed in August 1917 from the Home Service Garrison Battalions of 18 Regiments. It was made up of old soldiers who were beyond the age set for combatant service, or those who were not fit for duty overseas, sometimes as the result of wounds received on active service. The Corps was similar in some ways to the Home Guard of the Second

World War. The main job was to guard railways, tunnels, roads and ports, thus relieving other troops for front line service.

Whether Thomas served previously with another battalion in unknown, but in 1911 he lived at 6 High Grange with his widowed father John and his sister Frances. At this time he was 25 years of age and a joiner. Because of his age he may have served with another battalion and because of injury or other issue been unfit for active service. The other alternative is that he may have been unfit for army service when he was conscripted, but he was called up to serve in the Royal Defence Corps after it was formed in 1917. Thomas was promoted to Sergeant, but no army records have survived.

Bob Worthy, Royal Field Artillery (Army Veterinary Corps)

Bob was born in Croxdale, Durham between July and September 1881. In 1907 he married Agnes and by 1911, he was working as a stud groom for Henry Stobart of Witton Towers and living at 5 West End, Witton le Wear. Bob and Agnes had one child who died prior to 1911.

Bob joined the Army on the 14th July 1915 at Darlington, and was 5ft 3½inches tall, weighed 125 lbs. and had a 37 inch chest. His physical development was good although he did have flat feet.   On the 1st August he arrived at Le Havre in France.   Being used to working with horses, it seems appropriate that he was serving with the Army Veterinary Corps which was part of the 28th Battalion of the Royal Field Artillery. He would have seen a great deal of frontline activity and during his 3 years and 4 months in France, he was given 3 periods of leave enabling him to return home to his family. These were from the 30th December 1915 until 6th January 1916, 24th June

1917 until 4th July 1917, 15th October until 30th October 1918, but this was extended until 3rd November 1918. He finally left France for demobilisation on the 20th March 1919. Bob was promoted to Sergeant on the 6th May 1918. He was discharged into the Army Reserve on the 19th April 1919 and it was recorded that he had a weak left knee, the outcome of being kicked by a mule in July 1916. This was classed as a disability as he had joint swelling and suffered pain at his discharge medical in March 1919.

Lance Walton, 1/6th Durham Light Infantry

Lancelot Younghusband Walton was born in 1896, the eldest son of William and Elizabeth Walton. At the age of 15, Lance was working underground as a coal mine driver, possibly in the same pit as his coal hewer father. In 1911, the family were living at 27 High Grange, North Bitchburn.

Lance joined up in May 1915 at Bishop Auckland with the 3rd Battalion Durham Light Infantry. His medical indicated he was 5ft 8¼inches tall, had a 38 inch chest and was in good health. He was appointed Lance Corporal with the 2nd DLI on the 21st January 1916 and was posted to the 1st DLI on the 7th July 1916 where he was sent to France to join the British Expeditionary Force. In 1917 he was serving as a saddler and received extra pay for this duty. Lance came home on leave for 2 weeks from the 19th November 1917 until the 5th December 1917. On the night of the 9/10th August 1918, Lance was admitted to 56 General Hospital at Etaples with a gunshot wound in his left heel, but was well enough to rejoin his unit on 6th September 1918. He had a further leave to the UK on the 11th October 1918 until the 22nd October 1918.

Lance's home address on demobilisation on the 1st January 1919 was 18 High Street, Howden le Wear and he was awarded the Victory and British War medals.

Witton le Wear and its Memorials

Witton le Wear is situated in rural County Durham, straddling the A68, 5.5 miles from Bishop Auckland and 15 miles from Durham City. It is a historic village and has had people living in the area since Anglo Saxon times. The village played its part in the English Civil War (1642 – 1649) and some of its current houses can be traced back to this time. Industrialisation came to the area in the 19th century and the population in the parish rose in its heyday to 2,630 in 1891. Employment was mainly in the North Bitchburn Coal Company at Howden Colliery, the Wear Valley Brick Works, and the Witton Fire Brick Company all of which made fire bricks, sanitary pipes and ornamental wares. George Langstaff and Sons, supported employment in the local sawmills. Farm labourers also worked in the surrounding farms. At the turn of the 20th century, Witton le Wear supported three churches, 3 drift mines, five public houses, a railway station, a school, six shops, a watermill, a sawmill and the castle. There are currently just over 500 residents, two churches, two public houses, a primary school and the community centre remaining as the social heart of the village.

The Parish Church of St Philip and St James is situated at the centre of the village and on the original site of its 12th century Norman predecessor. If you enter the church, on the interior wall facing towards the porch, is situated the village war memorial. It takes the form of two brass plates, one dedicated to the First World War and a smaller one dedicated to the Second World War.

Immediately after the end of the war in 1918, battlefield pilgrims and families of the fallen wanted to visit the battlegrounds and cemeteries particularly around the Somme and northern France. In 1919, the YMCA provided a very modest seventeen bed hostel giving bed and breakfast on the outskirts of Ypres, but by 1920 there were many more establishments offering accommodation, many provided by the Salvation Army or other charities. From June 1920, Thomas Cook advertised tours of the Western Front at a starting price of £8. 11s. and the South Eastern and Chatham Railway Company offered a two night stay with food and travel for £15.15s. This cost was often out of reach for the families from the North East and only the affluent could afford this luxury.

Many families grieved after the war and found it difficult as they had no grave or memorial to visit to remember their loved ones and as a result, memorials appeared in towns and villages.   Many were funded by public subscription, by employers or individuals and they took various forms e.g. memorial halls, monuments, plaques, lych gates etc.

On the 5th February 1924, a meeting of the St Philip and St James Parochial Church Council was held in the Sunday school building at the bottom of Cemetery Bank. Mr Temple raised the question of erecting a village memorial in memory of those who had lost their lives in the Great War. He suggested that a tablet be placed in the church with the names of the fallen inscribed thereon. Mr Tymms, the Council Secretary and minute taker, was also the head master of the village Board School, objected to the idea of a brass tablet as disfiguring, and pointing out the difficulty of refusing anyone else placing one in the church,' no matter how common or ugly'. Major Rudyard thought a bronze tablet would be a suitable memorial and would be unique and quite different from a tablet in memory of a private individual. Mr Temple moved that a tablet be placed in the church and that subscriptions be asked for that object. Mr Tymms moved an amendment that the Council agree that a memorial be placed in the church but the form it should take be settled at a later meeting. The amendment was carried and Mr Temple withdrew his motion.

A special meeting of the Council was held on the 19th February 1924 to discuss further the memorial. Twelve members were present. Mr Temple proposed that a circular be sent to every home in the parish to ask for subscriptions for a tablet which would cost about £30. Any money in excess could be donated to local hospitals. Major Rudyard agreed bronze tablet would be suitable at a cost of £30 - £40 and the letter should go to non-conformists as well as church members. He suggested that any additional money should be used to provide a memorial hall in the village. Mr Tymms proposed a stained glass window costing about £150 would be more appropriate, would offend no one's taste and be more in a public nature than a bronze tablet. After a vote, Mr Temple's motion was carried by one vote to allow a letter to go to every household to ask for subscriptions towards a tablet.

What happened over the next two months is not known but at the Parochial Church Council meeting on the 24th April 1924, there was a note in the minutes stating that

'There was a suggestion that a War Memorial should be erected in the Church under the auspices of the Church Council, but the memorial seems to have fallen through. The Parish Council has offered to take the matter in hand.'

It appears that the Parish Council managed to have the memorial, consisting of a brass plaque, erected in the Church at a later date. There are no records available of how the memorial was funded or of the date it was consecrated in the church, but this would have happened soon after it was erected. The plaque was of a standard design as recommended by the Imperial War Graves Commission. A second brass plate, funded by the local branch of the Women's Institute, was added following World War II.

Wolsingham Grammar School Memorial

At Wolsingham Grammar School, the secondary school for Weardale, the very first Great War memorial in Britain was established. It was decided to plant an oak sapling to the memory of every one of the former pupils who died during the war. On a damp March morning in 1918, 18 oaks were dedicated and during the summer term of 1919, more trees were planted to remember other former pupils who died after March 1918. Amongst the memorial trees dedicated were two to the memory of Alexander Lister Richardson and Harry Langstaff, both Witton le Wear men. A brass plate can still be seen beside the trees with the inscription:

THE MEMORIAL OAKS
These trees were planted in memory of Old Boys
who fell in the Great War
'Non timidi pro patria mori'

There is also a formal war memorial situated within the school which was unveiled on the 16th March 1922. It is a dark oak frame with photographs of all the Old Boys who died and an illuminated panel with the names and the school coat of arms. Every year on the 11th November, Wolsingham School pupils and teachers take great pride in paying their respects to these young men who fell in the Great War.

Living in Witton le Wear 1914 – 1919

The parish magazine for St Philip and St James Church for October 1979 contained an article written by Miss Ramshaw who had been born in Witton le Wear, and whose family had lived in the village for generations, reflecting on life prior to World War I. It provides a wonderful picture of the village at the outbreak of war.

'The Vicar at that time was the Reverend James Hodgson, who was responsible for the present church building. Although almost 90 years old, his hearing was good and he did not need spectacles. The Vicarage in Station Road [now a private house] was a low whitewash building. A flight of steps led down to the front door and I remember a pump in the middle of the kitchen floor from which water was drawn. There were also two pumps in the village, one on the green and one near the Sunday School. This building had been the Day School in the early part of the 19th century. [This is now a private house at the bottom of Cemetery Bank]. The Sunday School was supervised by Miss Mary Jopling for many years, but Reverend Hodgson refused to have anything to do with it or Miss Jopling. There is a memorial window dedicated to her in the north wall of the church. The Reverend Hodgson and his wife can be seen in the window to the right of the Altar, with the old vicarage and the new Church in the background.

What was life like in Witton at that time? We had four general shops, also a butcher, a tailor, a baker, a joiner, a cobbler, a fish and chip shop and a blacksmith's forge. Wear Terrace had its own small shop. Work was provided by two drift mines, a sawmill, brickworks and a quarry. The Castle and Tower estates also employed many people.

Although we had no buses, there was a very good train service, and for many years Witton le Wear won the prize for the best kept station: the flower beds were beautiful. Having no radio or television, how did we know the time? By the station clock, the sawmill buzzer and the ringing of the school bell.

In the winter we could sledge from the Tower gates to the bottom of Clemmy Bank, also from the Cemetery to the station. Baskets of apples were thrown on the green in the autumn for which the children scrambled. The fields and hedges were full of wild flowers and the riverside provided all we needed for enjoyment in the summer, apart from our day trip to the seaside. Yes, life was slow, but oh, it was good.'

Miss Ramshaw

There is no doubt village life in Witton le Wear had a good community spirit. Cars and mechanical vehicles were rare and horses and carts provided most of the transport. Villagers worked and lived locally and children were schooled in the village.

Education

The Education Act of 1870 provided formal education for children and the 1880 Act made school attendance mandatory for children up to the age of 10 years of age. Board schools could insist that children attended between the ages of 5 and 13. It was not until 1918 that the compulsory school age was raised to 14 years of age. The Board School (the current Community Centre) was erected in 1874 and could accommodate 220 pupils. The school master's residence was attached to the school building. It was in continual use until 1968 when the new school was built in St James Gardens. Children who showed promise could gain a scholarship to Grammar Schools in Bishop Auckland or Wolsingham and children of wealthier parents could be educated at private school.

Churches

St Philip and St James Parish Church was by the end of the 19th century in ruins and had lost its roof in a fire. The church was repaired and re-consecrated in 1902. Reverend James Francis Hodgson was vicar from 1878 until 1922.

The first Primitive Methodist Chapel was erected in 1850 and could seat 350 worshipers. At the turn of the century the church size proved to be inadequate and it was enlarged by building a new church on top of the existing structure.

The Wesleyan Methodist Chapel could seat 250 people and when demolished in 1965, the organ was moved to the Primitive Methodist Chapel on the opposite side of the village green.

Railway

The railway station, built in 1889 on the eastern side of the level crossing had sidings, and a goods shed. It replaced the original station house which was built in 1847, but being on a bend in the line, became unsuitable for expansion. On the eastern side of the level crossing were coal staithes. A cattle dock and siding were located on the west side of the crossing, below the Railway Hotel, now a private house. The house at the railway crossing was built in 1847 for the crossing keeper and the Stockton and Darlington railway plaque can still be seen on the side of the cottage.

Shops and Public Houses

Marshall's the cobblers was situated above the Post Office which was at the top of Post Office Street. Baker's the drapers, Brown's general store and Gill's the butchers were all found in Station Road. Bowen's shop and Carney's general dealers were in the centre of the village.

The Railway Hotel was near the level crossing and the Mason's Arms was in School Street. The Victoria Hotel was a thriving establishment in the centre of the village and it was established prior to 1850. It is one of the two public houses still in existence. The Gray Mare was situated on the A68 and Thomas Jolly was the landlord until he died in 1912. The Dun Cow was established in 1799 and has been in continuous use as a public house for over 200 years. The Bay Horse was on the outskirts of the village at the top of Hargill Bank near Howden le Wear.

Attack on Witton le Wear

The Auckland Chronicle on the 22nd July 1916 ran the following story.

"About 7 o'clock on Thursday night last, a starting contretemps occurred, when the villagers turned out en masse when disturbed by the news that an

aeroplane was to be seen hovering over the village. Nervous people possessed of cellars fled in frantic haste to their protective bases, only to be made aware shortly afterwards by a closer scrutiny of the aerial object that it was not a bomb dropping 'Germhun' flying sausage; but merely a harmless kite of rather abnormal size."

As Miss Ramshaw recorded – life in Witton le Wear was good.

Witton le Wear Poem

A poem written about Witton le Wear was uncovered in 2000. Its author is unknown, but its style of prose is suggestive of the late 19th century. The words encompass what many of our soldiers would have felt about their home and has been used to head the soldier's stories.

Appendix I

Commonwealth War Graves Commission

Sir Fabian Ware arrived in France in 1914 as Commander of the British Red Cross which took upon itself the task to record and care for the final resting place of casualties. In 1915, this work was given official recognition and became the Graves Registration Commission, in 1917 renamed the Imperial War Graves Commission and in 1960 became the Commonwealth War Graves Commission.

In 1915, the government had placed a blanket ban on the repatriation of the remains of any soldier and this ban remained in place after the end of hostilities. The Commission and the government agreed that the finest memorial to the dead would be that they should be left together, regardless of rank and class, in the country where they died. The Times newspaper[36], with government and Commission backing, ran the following report.

"Comradeship in death, soldier's bodies not to be brought home

> The removal of bodies to their native countries is strongly desired by the relatives of a small number of cases but the reasons against this course appeared to the Commission to be overwhelming. To allow removal by a few individuals (of necessity only those who could afford the cost) would be contrary to the principle of equality of treatment; to empty some of the 400,000 identified graves would be a colossal work and would be opposed to the spirit in which the Empire gratefully accepted the offers made by the Governments of France, Belgium, Italy and

---

[36] Times Newspaper 29th November 1918

Greece to provide land in perpetuity for our cemeteries and to 'adopt' our dead... The evidence available to the Commission confirmed their conviction that the dead themselves in whom the sense of comradeship was so strong, would have preferred to lie with their comrades."

On the request of bereaved families, photographs of the graves were taken and sent to the relatives and by 1917 over 12,000 photographs had been dispatched. They were given a Royal Charter in 1917 and became the Imperial War Graves Commission.

Three eminent architects, Sir Edwin Lutyens, Sir Herbert Baker and Sir Reginald Blomfield designed cemeteries and memorials which "would commemorate in perpetuity the sacrifice of the Empire's soldiers." (Winston Churchill 1920[37]) By the spring of 1921, over 1,000 cemeteries had been established and deemed fit to receive visitors. Families could at last officially travel to visit the graves of their sons, husbands and fathers. As so many men were lost without trace, between 1923 and 1938, numerous memorials were built in France and Flanders to commemorate this sacrifice; the largest being at Thiepval which carries the names of over 72,000 soldiers who died at the Battle of the Somme in 1916 and have no known grave.

After WWII, the Commission took on construction work to commemorate a further 600,000 Commonwealth war dead and in 1960 the name was changed to the Commonwealth War Graves Commission.

The Commission has paid tribute to over 1,700,000 men and women of Commonwealth forces who are now commemorated

---

[37] Winston Churchill, 4 May 1920, House of Commons

at military and civil sites in some 150 countries. It is a non-profit-making organisation and its core principles are:

- each of the dead should be commemorated by name on the headstone or memorial
- headstones and memorials should be permanent
- headstones should be uniform
- there should be no distinction made on account of military or civil rank, race or creed

Since its inception, the Commission has constructed 2,500 war cemeteries and plots, erecting headstones over graves and, in instances where the remains are missing, inscribing the names of the dead on permanent memorials.

There is one Commonwealth War Grave in Witton le Wear Cemetery. John Teasdale Craig DFM was a Battle of Britain Ace pilot who shot down at least 8 enemy planes. He was killed in a training accident on the 2nd June 1941 and brought back to be buried in the village.

Visiting the CWGC website, (www.cwgc.co.uk) enables searches for people or cemeteries to be undertaken. Photographs and cemetery plans are available as well as directions how to reach the cemetery if a visit is planned.

Appendix II

WWI Campaign and Gallantry Medals

There were seven campaign medals awarded for those who served during WWI. Medals were issued automatically for other ranks, but officers or their families had to apply for them. Information was usually impressed around the rim of the medal and this could be all or some of the following: service number, rank, name, military unit.

1914 Star	Bronze medal authorised for those who served under enemy fire in France or Belgium, between 5th August 1914 and 22nd November 1914. There were over 378,000 1914 stars issued.
1914 – 1915 Star	Bronze medal awarded to all who served in any theatre of war against Germany between 5th August 1914 and 31st December 1915, excluding those eligible for the 1914 star, the Africa General Service Medal or the Sudan 1910 Medal. An estimated 2.4 million 1914 – 1915 stars were distributed. The medal was nick-named 'pip'
British War Medal	Silver or bronze medal awarded to officers and men of the British and Imperial Forces who either served in a theatre of war or service overseas between 5th August 1914 and 11th November 1918 inclusive. Approximately 6.5 million British War Medals were distributed. The medal was nick-named 'squeak'.
The Allied Victory Medal	Each of the allies issued their own bronze Victory medal with similar design and wording. Approximately 5.7 million Victory medals were issued. The British medal was nick-named 'wilfred'.
Territorial Force War Medal	Only members of the Territorial Force and Territorial Force Nursing Service were eligible for this medal and they must have been members of the Territorial Force before 30 September 1914 and served in an operational war zone outside of the UK between 5th August 1914 and 11th November 1918. Approximately 34,000 medals were issued.
The Silver War Badge	This sterling silver badge was issued to officers and men who were discharged or retired from military service as a result of sickness or injury caused by war service. After April 1918, the eligibility was amended to include civilians serving with the Royal Army Medical Corps, female nurses, staff and aid workers. Approximately 1,150,000 Silver War Badges were issued for WWI service.
Mercantile Marine War Medal	The Board of Trade awarded this campaign medal to Merchant Navy servicemen who had made a voyage through a war or danger zone. 133,135 medals were awarded

There were a number of awards which individuals received for conspicuous and gallant acts of valour, usually in the presence of the enemy, whilst serving in the British and Commonwealth armed forces. There were awards also issued for distinguished and meritorious service.

The following awards are listed below in order of precedence:

Victoria Cross (VC)	The V.C. is the highest award for gallantry and awarded for an act of outstanding courage or devotion to duty in the presence of the enemy. All ranks were, and still are, eligible when serving with the British and Commonwealth armed forces. 615 V.C.s were awarded during WWI.
Distinguished Service Order (DSO)	The D.S.O was awarded for acts of meritorious or distinguished service in wartime, usually when under fire or in the presence of the enemy. Initially for officers ranked Major and above but was modified to include other officers including those of Royal Navy and after April 1918, the Royal Air Force. During WWI, 9000 DSO's were awarded.
Distinguished Service Cross (DSC)	The D.S.C. was awarded to naval officers below the rank of Lieutenant Commander for gallantry at sea in the presence of the enemy. Almost 2,000 D.S.C.s were awarded during the WW1.
Military Cross (MC)	The Military Cross was a decoration for gallantry during active operations in the presence of the enemy. Commissioned officers with the rank of Captain or below or Warrant Officer were eligible for the award. From June 1917 officers of the rank of captain but who had a temporary rank of major could also receive the award. 37,081 military crosses were awarded for service during WW1, plus 2,992 first Bars, 176 second Bars and 4 third Bars.
Distinguished Flying Cross (DFC)	The D.F.C was awarded to officers and warrant officers of the Royal Air Force for an act or acts of valour, courage or devotion to duty while flying on active operations against the enemy. During WW1 there were about 1,100 D.F.C. awards.
Air Force Cross (AFC)	The award was given to personnel of the British Armed Forces and other Commonwealth Forces for an act or acts of valour, courage or devotion to duty whilst flying though not in active operations against the enemy. Officers and Warrant Officers were eligible for the award.
Distinguished Conduct Medal (DCM)	The D.C.M. was awarded for gallantry in the field in the face of the enemy. Other ranks in the British Army and also non-commissioned ranks in Commonwealth Forces were eligible for this award.

Conspicuous Gallantry Medal (CGM)	The C.G.M. was awarded to other ranks for an act of gallantry against the enemy at sea or in the air.
Distinguished Service Medal (DSM)	The D.S.M was awarded for bravery whilst on active service at sea and was for other ranks Royal Navy personnel, members of the other Services and other Commonwealth countries who held rank up to and including Chief Petty Officer.
Military Medal (MM)	The Military Medal was awarded to other ranks of the British Army and Commonwealth Forces. It was an award for gallantry and devotion to duty when under fire in battle on land.
Distinguished Flying Medal (DFM)	The DFM was awarded to other ranks of the Royal Air Force for an act or acts of valour, courage or devotion to duty while flying on active operations against the enemy. Later it was available to the equivalent ranks in the Army and Royal Navy for acts of valour in the air.
Air Force Medal (AFM)	The award was given to personnel of the British Armed Forces and other Commonwealth Forces for an act or acts of valour, courage or devotion to duty whilst flying though not in active operations against the enemy. Other ranks were eligible for the award

Mentioned in Dispatches

To be 'mentioned in dispatches' was a commendation of an act of gallantry. These were published in the London Gazette and led to the phrase 'being gazetted' as being in a newspaper article.

Death of a Serviceman

If a member of the armed forces perished during the war, the next of kin were offered the medals posthumously. They were also sent a memorial plaque which was a 121mm circular bronze disc. Over 1 million plaques were produced and sent to the next of kin at the end of the war and was colloquially known as 'The Dead Man's Penny'.

The Secretary of State for War was also instructed on behalf of the King to send a letter to every family of a serviceman killed in action. A copy of this letter can be seen in the images and photographs of Private Scott.

Appendix III

Who lived where?

It is interesting to look at the homes where it was recorded that the servicemen lived. Many of the addresses are still private homes today. Where the house number is known it is included.

West End and Quarry (A68)

Gerard Sadler	Briardale, Witton le Wear
Robert Worthy	5 West End, Witton le Wear
William Marr	7 West End, Witton le Wear
Bertram Randall	11 West End, Witton le Wear
John Lowson	14 West End, Witton le Wear and Marshall Green Farm
Robert Moreland	17 West End, Witton le Wear
George Vasey	20 West End, Witton le Wear
John Darbyshire	Witton Freestone Quarry
Benjamin Darbyshire	Witton Freestone Quarry

Carr's Terrace and High Street

Stephen Binks	Carr's Terrace, Witton le Wear
Jack Todd	5 High Street, Witton le Wear
William Henderson	12, High Street, Witton le Wear
Herbert Roper	Witton Towers, Witton le Wear
John Stobart	Witton Towers, Witton le Wear
Frederick Hall	Victoria House, Witton le Wear
Edmund Coates	18 High Street, Witton le Wear
Henry Heslop	Pear Tree House, Witton le Wear
Geoffrey Purson	Witton House, Witton le Wear

Cemetery Road, Cemetery Bank and Hill House Farm

John Oddy	2 Cemetery Road, Witton le Wear
Robert Brooksbank	5 Cemetery Road, Witton le Wear
George Laverick	4 Cemetery Bank, Witton le Wear
Edward Hogg	Cemetery Bank, Witton le Wear
Joseph Armstrong	14 Cemetery Bank, Witton le Wear
Thomas W Allinson	Hill House Farm, Witton le Wear

Post Office Street

Albert Brown	11 Post Office Street, Witton le Wear
Robert Laverick	19 Post Office Street, Witton le Wear

Railway Terrace

Benjamin Heslop	2 Railway Terrace, Witton le Wear
George Peacock	8 Railway Terrace, Witton le Wear
Anthony Jackson	9 Railway Terrace, Witton le Wear
Joe Jackson	9 Railway Terrace, Witton le Wear

Wear Terrace

William Allinson	Wear Terrace, Witton le Wear
John Stobbs	Wear Terrace, then 6 West End, Witton le Wear
Joseph Stobbs	Wear Terrace, then 6 West End, Witton le Wear
Thomas Stobbs	Wear Terrace, then 6 West End, Witton le Wear
Charles Robson	7 Wear Terrace, Witton le Wear
Thomas Ward	11 Wear Terrace, Witton le Wear

Station Road

Joseph Proud	9 Station Road, Witton le Wear
Joseph Brown	12 Station Road, Witton le Wear
Richard Langstaff	16 Station Road, Witton le Wear
Harry Langstaff	Laburnum House, Witton le Wear
Henry Stephenson	21 Station Road , Witton le Wear
Edward Heslop	25 Station Road, Witton le Wear
Frederick Proud	26 Station Road, Witton le Wear
Thomas Bainbridge	31 Station Road, Witton le Wear
John Bainbridge	31 Station Road, Witton le Wear
Robert Bainbridge	31 Station Road, Witton le Wear
Frederick Brown	Station Road, Witton le Wear

School Street and Witton Castle

John Richards	Victoria Hotel, Witton le Wear
Robert Richards	Victoria Hotel, Witton le Wear
Walter Gillard	3 School Street, and Witton Castle Lodge House
George Jamieson	8 School Street, Witton le Wear
John Potts	9 School Street, Witton le Wear
George Walton Scott	10 School Street, Institute House, Witton le Wear
Thomas Potts	12 School Street, Witton le Wear
William Rutter	Gate House, Witton Castle
Arthur Rutter	Gate House, Witton Castle

Some of the servicemen lived outside the immediate village but in the surrounding areas.

Bishop Auckland

Albert Dean	53 Newgate Street, Clarence Villas and 13 Newgate St. Bishop Auckland,

Harperley

Alexander Richardson	Harperley Post Office then Chester le Street

North Bitchburn, Howden le Wear and Roddymoor

Ralph Carr	North Bitchburn
Lance Walton	27 High Grange, North Bitchburn
James Coates	Constantine Road and 8 Low Row, North Bitchburn
Stephen Carr	Low Row 10, North Bitchburn
Christopher Whitton	Valley Terrace, Howden le Wear and Red House, Roddymoor

Witton Park

John Sanders	6 Black Road, Witton Park

Local addresses of two of the men listed in the war memorial are not known.

A Smith
Henry Maguire

Appendix IV

Regiments the men served with

Soldiers are traditionally very proud of the regiments they serve with. Many of our men would have desired to serve with their local county regiment, the Durham Light Infantry, but this was not always possible and they were ordered to go to the regiment that needed them most. This may because of skills they possessed, or for operational need.

It is reassuring that some soldiers from the village served and fought alongside men they possibly knew in peacetime although in some cases brothers fought for different regiments. The men from Witton le Wear served in a variety of regiments during WWI.

Army Service Corp

A Smith	Army Service Corp	Regimental Number unknown
George Vasey	Army Service Corp	Regimental Number 357140

Border Regiment

Joe Jackson	Army Cyclist Corp (Border Regiment)	Regimental Number 6930
Edward Heslop	5th Battalion, Border Regiment	Regimental Number 18492
Thomas Bainbridge	9th Battalion, Border Regiment	Regimental Number 13066
Albert Brown	9th Battalion, Border Regiment	Regimental Number 13069
Frederick Brown	9th Battalion, Border Regiment	Regimental Number 13112
George Peacock	9th Battalion, Border Regiment	Regimental Number 9/14282
Arthur Rutter	9th Battalion, Border Regiment	Regimental Number 15642

| Jack Todd | 9th Battalion, Border Regiment | Regimental Number 18640 |
| Thomas Potts | Border Regiment and 23rd Northumberland Fusiliers | Regimental Numbers 14271 and 64446 |

Coldstream Guards

Ralph Carr	2nd Battalion, Coldstream Guards	Regimental Number 18681
Thomas Stobbs	3rd Battalion, Coldstream Guards	Regimental Number 19415
Anthony Jackson	3rd Battalion, Coldstream Guards	Regimental Number 22789

Durham Light Infantry

Robert Moreland	DLI	Regimental Number 18/1538
Edward Hogg	2nd Battalion, DLI	Regimental Number 3/9891
John Sanders	2nd Battalion, DLI	Regimental Number 73310
John Bainbridge	4th Battalion DLI	Regimental Number 73954
Robert Bainbridge	4th Battalion, DLI	Regimental Number 95504
Robert Brooksbank	5th Battalion, DLI	Regimental Number 95486
Walter Gillard	6th Battalion DLI	Regimental Numbers 6/2545 and 203230
Christopher Whitton	6th Battalion, DLI	Regimental Number 250437
Lance Walton	6th Battalion, DLI	Regimental Number 250436
Harry Langstaff	6th Battalion DLI and 13th DLI	Regimental number 100336.
Robert Richards	8th Battalion DLI	Regimental Number 32299
John Stobbs	15th Battalion DLI	Regimental Number 19880
Alexander Richardson	18th Battalion DLI	Regimental Number 18/579
Joseph Stobbs	18th Battalion DLI	Regimental Number 1007
Albert Dean	29th Battalion DLI, Royal Engineers, 126th Field Coy	Regimental Number 80475
John Lowson	DLI and 9th West Yorkshire Reg.	Regimental Number 23750
William Marr	DLI and Machine Gun Corp	Regimental Numbers 12726 and 20081

Dragoon Guards

Gerard Sadler   3rd Battalion Dragoon Guards   Regimental Number unknown

East Yorkshire Regiment

William Rutter   8th Battalion East Yorkshire Regiment   Regimental Number 13301

Richard Langstaff   East Yorkshire Regiment and Lincoln Regiment   Regimental Numbers 37142 and 44067

Kings Royal Rifle Corps

Frederick Hall   1st Battalion, Kings Royal Rifle Corps   Regimental Number C/12776

Kings Own Yorkshire Light Infantry

William Allinson   10th Battalion Kings Own Yorkshire LI   Regimental Number 35043

Lancashire Fusiliers

Charles Robson   19th Battalion Lancashire Fusiliers   Regimental number 34439

Manchester Regiment

George Jamieson   3rd Manchester Regiment   Regimental Number 76557

Military Foot Police

Herbert Roper   Military Foot Police   Regimental Number 83682

Northumberland Fusiliers

Bertram Randall	1st Battalion, Northumberland Fusiliers	Regimental Number 1492
Henry Heslop	6th Battalion, Northumberland Fusiliers	Regimental Number C/18775

Royal Army Medical Corp

Joseph Brown	Royal Army Medical Corp	Regimental Number 24085

Royal Defence Corp

Thomas Ward	Royal Defence Corp	Regimental Number 65034

Royal Engineers

Stephen Carr	Royal Engineers	Regimental Number 251970 Coldstream Guards 17383
Henry Maguire	Royal Engineers	Regimental Number 142071
Edmund Coates	Royal Engineers	Regimental Number 145626
John Darbyshire	Royal Engineers	Regimental Number 354416
William Henderson	Royal Engineers	Regimental Number 298306
James Coates	Royal Engineers, 255th Tunnelling Coy	Regimental Number 197785

Royal Field Artillery

Benjamin Darbyshire	Royal Field Artillery	Regimental Number 231878
John Stobart	Royal Field Artillery	Regimental Number unknown
Robert Worthy	Royal Field Artillery	Regimental Number 10871

Royal Fusiliers

John Oddy	28th Battalion Royal Fusiliers	Regimental Number 95908

Royal Garrison Artillery

George Laverick	Royal Garrison Artillery	Regimental Number 99449
John Richards	Royal Garrison Artillery	Regimental Number 337772
Frederick Proud	Royal Garrison Artillery	Regimental Number 283680
John Potts	Royal Garrison Regiment	Regimental Number 5406
Henry Stephenson	Royal Garrison Regiment	Regimental Number 152005

South Lancashire Regiment

George Walton Scott	South Lancashire Regiment	Regimental Number 34510

West Yorkshire Regiment

Joseph Armstrong	West Yorkshire Regiment	Regimental Number 60194 Army Labour Corps 376077
Benjamin Heslop	West Yorkshire Regiment	Regimental Number 77556
Robert Laverick	West Yorkshire Regiment	Regimental Number 120965 West Yorks 45741
Thomas William Allinson	12th Battalion West Yorkshire Regiment	Army Labour Corp 631294
Joseph Proud	West Yorkshire Regiment and Agricultural Labour Corps	Regimental Numbers 77637 and 439927

Yorkshire Regiment

Stephen Binks   4th Battalion Yorkshire Regiment   Regimental Number 204746

Thomas Jackson   18th Battalion Yorkshire Regiment   Regimental Number 62998

48th Infantry Brigade

Geoffrey Purson   48th Infantry Brigade   Regimental Number unknown

Appendix V

References and resources

A History of the Commonwealth War Graves Commission. Published by CWGC. ISA 08/03

Ancestry.co.uk www.ancestry.co.uk

Arthur, Max. *Last Post.* Cassell

Brittain, Vera. *Vera Brittain's War Diary 1913 – 1917.* Victor Gollancz Ltd.,

Dyer, Geof, *The Missing of the Somme,* Phoenix Publishers 1994

Fitzgerald D.J.I, in *Anzio* by Lloyd Clark. Headline Publishing Group

Minutes of the Parish Church of St Philip and St James Parochial Council meetings. 5th February 1924, 19th February 1924, 24th April 1924. Durham County Record Office

National Archives, The WWI soldiers records and war diaries that survive are available at the National Archives at Kew, London. www.nationalarchives.gov.uk

North East War Memorials Project, The North East War Memorials Project is intended to assist the public, Local History Groups and Schools, to learn about and research their neighbourhood War Memorials, and record the results. http://www.newmp.org.uk

Parish Magazine of St Philip and St James, October 1979

Patch, Harry, *Forgotten Voices of the Great War.* Ebury Press, London

Royal Army Medical Corps Training Manual, 1911. The War Office 1914

Swinton Sir E. Collection, *Twenty Years After.* George Newnes Ltd. 1939

The Great War, Useful website, www.thegreatwar.co.uk

The History of Wolsingham Grammar School, Anita Atkinson. Linton Printers, Crook

The Long, Long Trail, Useful website. www.1914-1918.net

Van Emden, Richard. *The Quick and the Dead.* Bloomsbury Publications

Ward S. G. P, *Faithful – the story of the Durham Light Infantry.* Thomas Nelson and Sons

INDEX

About the Author

Anne Yuill, a Scot by birth, has lived in County Durham from 1975 and spent 40 years as a nurse, midwife, ward sister, health visitor and corporate services manager in the NHS. In 2011 she retired from paid employment and decided that she would divert some of her energy into her hobbies of genealogy and history. Anne has established a small business 'Relativity' that will help people carry out research into their own family histories and ensure that stories are recorded for posterity.

In 2012, Anne published her first book 'Biting the Bullet' a biography of Reg Tallentire, a native of County Durham who served his country during WWII in three Scottish Regiments and when demobbed returned to the family business in Bishop Auckland where he worked until he retired one month before his 70th birthday. His stories make excellent reading.

Anne is determined that the men who survived the Great War and those who made the ultimate sacrifice from the village of Witton le Wear will not be forgotten. Hopefully 'Witton Warriors' will go some way to achieve this aim. A book about Witton le Wear during 1939 – 1945 including information about the men who died during WWII is under development.

Anne is married to Kelso, has two sons Andrew and Gordon Nicol and has lived in Witton le Wear since 1998. Step children and grandchildren help make Anne and Kelso's home the centre of a very happy family life.